Calculus methods

The School Mathematics Project

REFERENCE

CAMBRIDGE
UNIVERSITY PRESS

Main authors   Simon Baxter
Stan Dolan
Doug French
Andy Hall
Barrie Hunt
Mike Leach
Tim Lewis
Lorna Lyons
Richard Peacock
Paul Roder
Jeff Searle
David Tall
Thelma Wilson
Phil Wood

Project director   Stan Dolan

The authors would like to give special thanks to Ann White for her help in producing the trial edition and in preparing this book for publication.

The publishers would like to thank the following for supplying photographs:

front cover – reproduced by permission of the Board of Trustees of the Victoria and Albert Museum;
page 79 – ESA/PLI/Science Photo Library;
Simon Fraser/Science Photo Library.

Published by the Press Syndicate of the University of Cambridge
The Pitt Building, Trumpington Street, Cambridge CB2 1RP
40 West 20th Street, New York, NY 10011–4211, USA
10 Stamford Road, Oakleigh, Melbourne 3166, Australia

First published 1992
Reprinted 1993

Cartoons by Tony Hall

Produced by Gecko Limited, Bicester, Oxon.

Cover design by Iguana Creative Design

Printed in Great Britain at the University Press, Cambridge

British Library cataloguing in publication data

A catalogue record for this book is available from the British Library.

ISBN 0 521 40892 X

Contents

1 Parameters

1.1 Curves which vary with time

Some people play golf in the comfort of their own homes by playing a golf simulation game on a computer.

A programmer who constructs such a game models the path of the ball as a spot moving across the screen. The path depends on the skill of the player, the choice of club and the power of the shot, together with an element of chance.

The screen can be thought of as a Cartesian (x, y) plane with the origin at the bottom left-hand corner of the screen.

Suppose the spot moves so that, t seconds after it is at the origin, $x = 2t$ and $y = t$.

(a) Plot (or sketch) the positions of the spot after 1, 2, 3, 4 and 5 seconds.

(b) Explain why the line with Cartesian equation $y = \frac{1}{2}x$ will pass through your five points.

(c) How could you change the equations to make the spot follow the same path as before, but at twice the speed?

(d) Plot the graphs from (a) and (c) on a computer or graphic calculator screen, using a **parametric graph plotter**. (The technology datasheet, *Parametric curve plotting*, will help you.)

The equations $x = 2t$ and $y = t$ are called **parametric equations** and the time, t, which determines the x- and y-coordinates, is called a **parameter**.

To plot a parametric curve, it is **sometimes** sufficient to 'plot some suitable points and join the dots', as in the following example.

EXAMPLE 1

Plot the curve given by the parametric equations:

$$x = 3t, \quad y = t^2 \quad \text{for } 0 \leqslant t \leqslant 3$$

SOLUTION

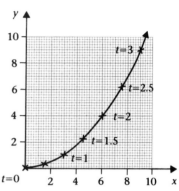

t	0	0.5	1	1.5	2	2.5	3
x	0	1.5	3	4.5	6	7.5	9
y	0	0.25	1	2.25	4	6.25	9

EXERCISE 1

1 (a) For the curve given by the parametric equations:

$$x = 20t, \quad y = 90 - 5t^2$$

complete the following table of values and plot the points on an (x, y) graph.

t	0	1	2	3	4	5
x						
y						

(b) On the same graph, plot the points which would arise if t were to take the values $-1, -2, -3, -4$ and -5. You should not need to recalculate the values – look for symmetry with your answers to part (a).

(c) What is the general shape of the curve?

2 By choosing suitable values of t and drawing up a table, plot the following parametric curves using any properties of symmetry or general shape to obtain the complete sketch.

(a) $x = 2t^2, \quad y = 4t^3$ (b) $x = 2t, \quad y = \dfrac{2}{t}$

Check your results using a graph plotter.

1.2 Circles and ellipses

In *Mathematical methods* you saw how Pythagoras' theorem can be used to show that the equation of a circle of radius r centred on the origin is:

$$x^2 + y^2 = r^2 \qquad ①$$

Introducing θ, the angle between OP and the x-axis, gives a different view of the problem.

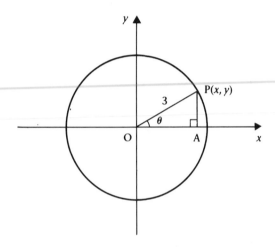

Consider a circle of radius 3.

You know that:

$$x^2 + y^2 = 9 \qquad \text{the Cartesian equation}$$

Using trigonometry and triangle OAP gives the parametric equations:

$$x = 3 \cos \theta, \quad y = 3 \sin \theta$$

(a) Describe what happens to x as θ varies.

(b) Describe what happens to y as θ varies.

(c) Explain why $(3 \cos \theta)^2 + (3 \sin \theta)^2 = 9$ for any value of θ and show how this connects the parametric and Cartesian equations of the circle.

TASKSHEET 1 — Ellipses (page 17)

For the **circle**, the Cartesian
equation is:
$$x^2 + y^2 = r^2$$

the parametric equations are:
$$x = r \cos \theta \quad y = r \sin \theta$$

and the area is πr^2.

For the **ellipse**, the Cartesian
equation is:

$$\frac{x^2}{a^2} + \frac{y^2}{b^2} = 1$$

the parametric equations are:

$$x = a \cos \theta, \quad y = b \sin \theta$$

and the area is $\pi a b$.

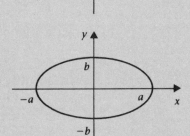

The major axis of the ellipse is of length $2a$ and its minor axis is
of length $2b$.

EXERCISE 2

1 Copy and complete the following table.

Ellipse	Cartesian equation	Parametric equations	Area
A	$\dfrac{x^2}{9} + \dfrac{y^2}{16} = 1$		
B		$x = 3 \cos \theta, \quad y = 5 \sin \theta$	
C	$\dfrac{x^2}{0.25} + \dfrac{y^2}{0.16} = 1$		

2 Rewrite $9x^2 + 4y^2 = 36$ in the form $\dfrac{x^2}{a^2} + \dfrac{y^2}{b^2} = 1$. Hence write down the
parametric equations and the area of this ellipse.

3 Repeat question 2 for the ellipse with equation $4x^2 + 25y^2 = 100$.

TASKSHEET 2E — Drawing parametric curves (page 19)

1.3 Conversion

In tasksheet 1, you saw how to convert the parametric equations:

$$x = a \cos \theta, \quad y = b \sin \theta$$

into the Cartesian equation:

$$\frac{x^2}{a^2} + \frac{y^2}{b^2} = 1$$

by using the trigonometric identity $\cos^2 \theta + \sin^2 \theta = 1$.

> Use the identity to convert the parametric equations $x = 5 \cos \theta$ and $y = 5 \sin \theta$ into the Cartesian equation $x^2 + y^2 = 25$.

Tasksheet 3 introduces two other trigonometric identities which are sometimes encountered in work on parametric equations.

TASKSHEET 3 — *Trigonometric ratios (page 20)*

$$\sec \theta = \frac{1}{\cos \theta}; \quad \operatorname{cosec} \theta = \frac{1}{\sin \theta}; \quad \cot \theta = \frac{1}{\tan \theta}$$

For any value of θ:

$$\cos^2 \theta + \sin^2 \theta = 1$$
$$1 + \tan^2 \theta = \sec^2 \theta$$
$$\cot^2 \theta + 1 = \operatorname{cosec}^2 \theta$$

You have used trigonometric identities to remove parameters from pairs of simultaneous equations. In general, conversion from parametric to Cartesian form involves the removal of a parameter using simultaneous equation techniques. Whilst these may involve indirect elimination using trigonometric identities, simpler direct methods are often used. This is illustrated in example 2.

E X A M P L E 2

Find the Cartesian equation of the curve given by the parametric equations:

$$x = 20t \qquad \text{①}$$
$$y = 90 - 5t^2 \qquad \text{②}$$

SOLUTION

Using equation ① to find t, $t = \dfrac{x}{20}$

Substituting for t in ②, $y = 90 - 5\left(\dfrac{x}{20}\right)^2 = 90 - \dfrac{x^2}{80}$

EXERCISE 3

1 Use algebra to find the Cartesian equation of the curve:

$$x = 2t - 1, \quad y = 4 - 2t$$

2 Find the Cartesian equations of:

(a) $x = 2 + 3t, \quad y = 4 - 5t$ (b) $x = 3t, \quad y = 5 - \dfrac{6}{t}$

(c) $x = 4t, \quad y = 10t - 5t^2$

3 Use appropriate trigonometric identities to find the Cartesian equations of:

(a) $2x = \sec \theta, \quad \dfrac{y}{3} = \tan \theta$ (b) $x = 4 \sin t, \quad y = 3 \cos t$

(c) $x = \operatorname{cosec} \theta, \quad y = \dfrac{1}{2} \cot \theta$ (d) $\dfrac{x}{3} = \sec \theta, \quad y = \tan \theta + 1$

4E For the parametric equations:

$$x = 1 + \sqrt{t}, \quad y = 4 + \sqrt{t}$$

(a) obtain the Cartesian equation.

(b) The curve given by the Cartesian equation is not quite the same as the curve given by the parametric equations. Why not?

5E

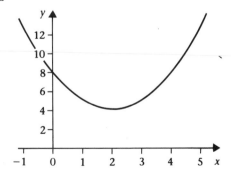

For the curve given by

$$y = (x - 2)^2 + 4$$

suggest two different possible sets of parametric equations.

1.4 Differentiating parametric equations

In *Mathematical methods* you used the chain rule to find rates of change in cases where there were two equations involving three variables.

> Use the chain rule to find $\dfrac{dy}{dx}$ when $y = \sin \theta$ and $\theta = 3x^2 + 2$.

Parametric equations can also give two equations with three variables. For example, a circle with centre the origin and radius 3 units has parametric equations:

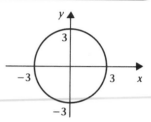

$$x = 3 \cos \theta, \quad y = 3 \sin \theta$$

In the thinking point you were able to find $\dfrac{dy}{dx}$ using the chain rule:

$$\frac{dy}{dx} = \frac{dy}{d\theta} \times \frac{d\theta}{dx}$$

because you could write down $\dfrac{dy}{d\theta}$ and $\dfrac{d\theta}{dx}$ from the given equations.

From the parametric equations, you can write down $\dfrac{dy}{d\theta}$ and $\dfrac{dx}{d\theta}$, but

not $\dfrac{d\theta}{dx}$. However, you should remember that $\dfrac{d\theta}{dx} = 1 \div \dfrac{dx}{d\theta}$.

This means that the chain rule can be rewritten as $\dfrac{dy}{dx} = \dfrac{dy}{d\theta} \div \dfrac{dx}{d\theta}$.

> (a) For the circle given by the parametric equations:
>
> $$x = 3 \cos \theta, \quad y = 3 \sin \theta$$
>
> use the formula $\dfrac{dy}{dx} = \dfrac{dy}{d\theta} \div \dfrac{dx}{d\theta}$ to show that:
>
> $$\frac{dy}{dx} = \frac{-\cos \theta}{\sin \theta}$$
>
> (b) Check that this answer gives the correct values for the gradient of the circle when $\theta = 0, \frac{1}{2}\pi$ and π.

E X A M P L E 3

For the curve defined parametrically by $x = 10t$, $y = 5t^2$,

find $\dfrac{dy}{dx}$ and the equation of the tangent to the (x, y) graph at $t = 3$.

S O L U T I O N

Differentiating, $\qquad \dfrac{dx}{dt} = 10 \quad$ and $\quad \dfrac{dy}{dt} = 10t$

$$\frac{dy}{dx} = \frac{dy}{dt} \div \frac{dx}{dt} = \frac{10t}{10} = t$$

When $t = 3$, $\quad \dfrac{dy}{dx} = 3$, $\quad x = 30 \quad$ and $\quad y = 45$.

The equation of the tangent is $\dfrac{y - 45}{x - 30} = 3 \quad$ or $\quad y = 3x - 45$.

E X E R C I S E 4

1   A curve has parametric equations $x = t$, $\quad y = \dfrac{1}{t}$. Write down $\dfrac{dx}{dt}$ and $\dfrac{dy}{dt}$

and hence find $\dfrac{dy}{dx}$. Calculate the gradient of the curve at $t = 2$.

2   A curve has parametric equations $x = 3 \cos \theta$, $\quad y = 4 \sin \theta$.
Work out the Cartesian coordinates and gradient at the point where $\theta = \frac{1}{2}\pi$.

3   For the curve defined by $x = 4u$, $\quad y = u^2$, find $\dfrac{dy}{dx}$ and the equation of the
tangent to the curve at the point where $u = 2$.

4   Find the equation of the tangent to the curve $x = u^2$, $\quad y = 2u^3$ at the point
where $u = 1$.

5   For the curve $x = 2v$, $\quad y = v^3 - 3v$:

(a) work out $\dfrac{dy}{dx}$;

(b) write down the two values of v for which $\dfrac{dy}{dx} = 0$;

(c) write down the x- and y-coordinates of the turning points on the curve.

1.5 Parametric differentiation or conversion?

In section 1.4, you used **parametric differentiaton** to find the gradients of curves given in parametric form. It might have occurred to you that you could have found some of the gradients by first converting the parametric equations to Cartesian equations. This may occasionally be an easy method. For example, if:

$$x = 2t + 3, \quad y = 6t + 9$$

you may spot at once that $y = 3x$, so $\dfrac{dy}{dx} = 3$.

Generally, however, parametric differentiation will be quicker.

E X A M P L E   4

A curve is defined by $x = 2t + 1, \quad y = t^2$.

(a) Use parametric differentiation to find the gradient at the point (5, 4).

(b) Find y in terms of x and so write down $\dfrac{dy}{dx}$ and find the gradient at the point (5, 4).

S O L U T I O N

(a) $\dfrac{dy}{dt} = 2t$ and $\dfrac{dx}{dt} = 2$, so $\dfrac{dy}{dx} = \dfrac{2t}{2} = t$

When $x = 5$ and $y = 4$, $t = 2$, so the gradient is 2.

(b) Since $x = 2t + 1, t = \dfrac{(x - 1)}{2}$

So $y = \dfrac{(x - 1)^2}{4}$

$\dfrac{dy}{dx} = \dfrac{2(x - 1)}{4} = \dfrac{(x - 1)}{2}$

When $x = 5$ the gradient is $\dfrac{4}{2} = 2$.

Even with this simple conversion, it is clear that parametric differentiation leads to a quicker solution, and there are many cases where the conversion is difficult or impossible.

EXERCISE 5

1   Given that $x = 3s$ and $y = s^2$, find $\dfrac{dy}{dx}$, first by parametric differentiation and then by conversion to a Cartesian equation.

Check that both methods give the same value for the gradient of the curve at $s = 1$.

2   For each part of this question, find $\dfrac{dy}{dx}$ by the method of your choice.

(a) $x = (t + 2)^2, \quad y = t^3 - 3$

(b) $x = 2t^2, \quad y = 6t^2 - 4$

(c) $x = 2\cos\theta - \sin\theta, \quad y = 3\sin\theta$

(d) $x = \sin 2\theta, \quad y = \sin 3\theta$

3E   Find the equation of the tangent to the curve $x = \theta - \cos\theta$, $y = \sin\theta$ at the point where $\theta = \frac{1}{4}\pi$. Write down the coordinates of the points A and B at which this tangent cuts the x- and y-axes respectively and hence find the area of the triangle OAB.

4E   A curve has parametric equations $x = t^2 + 4$ and $y = 2t^3 + 4t$.

(a) Find $\dfrac{dy}{dx}$ in terms of t and show that $\left(\dfrac{dy}{dx}\right)^2 \geqslant 12$.

(b) Sketch the curve.

1.6 Velocity vectors

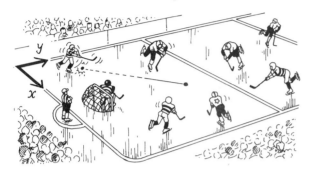

A puck is sliding across the ice with constant velocity. It starts on one side of the rink and its positions at the end of half-second intervals are given in the table.

Time, t seconds	0	0.5	1	1.5	2
Position vector, metres (from origin in corner of pitch)	$\begin{bmatrix} 0 \\ 6 \end{bmatrix}$	$\begin{bmatrix} 6 \\ 10.5 \end{bmatrix}$	$\begin{bmatrix} 12 \\ 15 \end{bmatrix}$	$\begin{bmatrix} 18 \\ 19.5 \end{bmatrix}$	$\begin{bmatrix} 24 \\ 24 \end{bmatrix}$

(a) Show on a graph that the points lie on a line.

(b) Find the Cartesian equation of this line.

(c) Find the velocity of the puck. Hence find its speed.

(d) Write expressions for x and y in terms of t. Differentiate these to find $\dot{x}$, i.e. $\dfrac{dx}{dt}$ and $\dot{y}$, i.e. $\dfrac{dy}{dt}$. What is the connection between these derivatives and the velocity, **v**, of the puck?

(e) Explain why both $\dfrac{dy}{dx}$ and $\dfrac{\dot{y}}{\dot{x}}$ represent the gradient of the line of points. What is the connection between the chain rule and the result:

$$\frac{dy}{dx} = \frac{\dot{y}}{\dot{x}}$$

If a moving particle has position vector $\mathbf{r} = \begin{bmatrix} x \\ y \end{bmatrix}$, then its velocity is given by $\mathbf{v} = \begin{bmatrix} \dot{x} \\ \dot{y} \end{bmatrix}$. The gradient of the velocity vector is:

$$\frac{dy}{dx} = \frac{\dot{y}}{\dot{x}}$$

E X A M P L E   5

A particle moves so that its position vector is given by:

$$\mathbf{r} = \begin{bmatrix} 2t + 2 \\ t^2 + 2t \end{bmatrix}$$

Plot the positions of the particle over the first three seconds and sketch its path. Calculate the velocity of the particle and mark the velocity vectors on the graph at $t = 0$ and $t = 2$.

S O L U T I O N S

t	0	1	2	3
$\mathbf{r}$	$\begin{bmatrix} 2 \\ 0 \end{bmatrix}$	$\begin{bmatrix} 4 \\ 3 \end{bmatrix}$	$\begin{bmatrix} 6 \\ 8 \end{bmatrix}$	$\begin{bmatrix} 8 \\ 15 \end{bmatrix}$

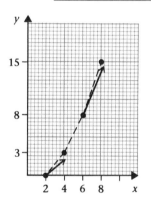

Differentiating, $\mathbf{v} = \begin{bmatrix} \dot{x} \\ \dot{y} \end{bmatrix} = \begin{bmatrix} 2 \\ 2t + 2 \end{bmatrix}$

When $t = 0$, $\mathbf{v} = \begin{bmatrix} 2 \\ 2 \end{bmatrix}$.   When $t = 2$, $\mathbf{v} = \begin{bmatrix} 2 \\ 6 \end{bmatrix}$

Notice that the velocity vectors are in the direction of the tangent to the curve. The lengths of the arrows indicate their magnitudes.

E X E R C I S E   6

1   For the position vector $\mathbf{r} = \begin{bmatrix} t^2 \\ 3t \end{bmatrix}$, find the coordinates of the points when

$t = 0, 1, 2$ and 3, and sketch the path. Differentiate to find the velocities when $t = 0, 1, 2$ and 3, and calculate their magnitudes. Mark each velocity on the curve using an arrow of appropriate length and direction.

2   The displacement in centimetres from the origin of a particle after t seconds is given by:

$$\mathbf{r} = \begin{bmatrix} 2 + t^2 \\ 3t - t^2 \end{bmatrix}$$

(a) Find the velocity after t seconds.

15

(b) Calculate its initial speed and direction (i.e. when $t = 0$).

(c) Find at what time it is travelling in the direction $\begin{bmatrix} 1 \\ 1 \end{bmatrix}$.

(d) When is it travelling parallel to the x-axis?

3 A particle moves along a straight line $y = 3x + 1$ with a constant speed of $\sqrt{10}$ units. What is the velocity vector?

   If the particle starts at $(0, 1)$ write down the position vector at time t.

After working through this chapter you should:

1 understand the word 'parameter' and recognise equations expressed in parametric form;

2 recognise the Cartesian and parametric forms of circles and ellipses;

3 be able to express equations written parametrically in Cartesian form and vice-versa;

4 be able to plot or sketch a curve given in parametric form;

5 know that:

$$\operatorname{cosec} \theta = \frac{1}{\sin \theta}; \quad \sec \theta = \frac{1}{\cos \theta}; \quad \cot \theta = \frac{1}{\tan \theta}$$

and be aware of the identities:

$$1 + \tan^2\theta = \sec^2\theta$$
$$1 + \cot^2\theta = \operatorname{cosec}^2\theta$$

6 be able to find the gradient of a curve expressed in parametric form;

7 be able to find the equation of a tangent to a curve expressed in parametric form;

8 be able to find the velocity vector of a particle whose position vector is given in terms of t (time).

Ellipses

1   Suppose a circle of radius 3 is stretched by a factor of 2 in the *x* direction so that the point P is transformed to P'.

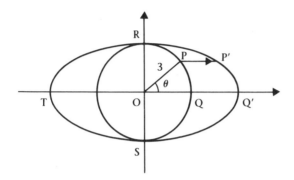

The resulting curve is known as an **ellipse**.

(a) Write down the coordinates of P in terms of θ.

(b) Write down the *y*-coordinate of P' in terms of θ.

(c) Write down the *x*-coordinate of P' in terms of θ.

(d) Write down the parametric equations of the ellipse.

(e) Write down the coordinates of R, Q and Q'.

TQ' is known as the **major axis** and SR is known as the **minor axis** of the ellipse.

(f) Write down the area of:

(i) the circle,

(ii) the ellipse.

2   (a) Sketch, on the same diagram, the curves:

(i) $x = 4 \cos \theta,\quad y = 4 \sin \theta$

(ii) $x = 5 \cos \theta,\quad y = 4 \sin \theta$

(b) The ellipse in (ii) can be obtained from the circle in (i) by means of a one-way stretch. What is the scale factor for this transformation?

(c) What is the area of:

(i) the circle,

(ii) the ellipse?

3 Sketch the graphs of the following curves, indicating the lengths of the major and minor axes.

(a) $x = 5 \cos \theta, \quad y = 6 \sin \theta$

(b) $x = 2 \cos \theta, \quad y = \sin \theta$

(c) $x = a \cos \theta, \quad y = b \sin \theta$

4 (a) Complete the following argument which leads to the Cartesian equation of an ellipse.

$$x = a \cos \theta, \quad y = b \sin \theta$$
$$\Rightarrow \cos \theta = ? \qquad \sin \theta = ?$$

So, since $\cos^2\theta + \sin^2\theta = ?$, it follows that

$$\left(\frac{?}{?}\right)^2 + \left(\frac{?}{?}\right)^2 = 1$$

or $\quad \dfrac{x^2}{?^2} + \dfrac{y^2}{?^2} = 1$

(b) Sketch the ellipse $\dfrac{x^2}{4} + \dfrac{y^2}{9} = 1$.

5 Consider the ellipse $\dfrac{x^2}{a^2} + \dfrac{y^2}{b^2} = 1$.

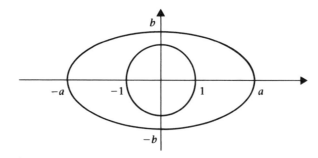

(a) This ellipse can be obtained from the circle $x^2 + y^2 = 1$ by means of a two-way stretch. What are the scale factors of this in the x and y directions?

(b) Write down the area of the circle $x^2 + y^2 = 1$. Hence write down the area of the ellipse.

Drawing parametric curves   *TASKSHEET* **2E**

1 (a) For the curve given by the parametric equations $x = \cos^3\theta$ and $y = \sin^3\theta$, complete the table and sketch the branch of the curve which is formed.

θ	0	$\frac{1}{6}\pi$	$\frac{1}{4}\pi$	$\frac{1}{3}\pi$	$\frac{1}{2}\pi$
x					
y					

   (b) How are the values of x and y for $\frac{1}{2}\pi < \theta \leqslant \pi$ related to the values in the table? Use these relationships to sketch the part of the curve $\frac{1}{2}\pi < \theta \leqslant \pi$.

   (c) Use symmetry properties to complete the sketch of the curve.

   (d) Check your curve using a graph plotter.

2 Sketch the curve given by:

$$x = \theta - \sin\theta, \quad y = 1 - \cos\theta$$

3 It is often possible to sketch a curve without plotting a large number of points. Consider, for example, the curve given by:

$$x = \frac{1 + t}{2 - t}, \quad y = \frac{2 + t}{4 - t}$$

   (a) Write down where the curve cuts the axes.

As $t \to 2$ from above, $2 - t$ is a small negative quantity, so $x \to -\infty$.
As $t \to 2$, $y \to 2$, so $y = 2$ is an asymptote.

   (b) Explain what happens as $t \to 2$ from below (i.e. through values smaller than 2).

   (c) Write down any further asymptotes.

   (d) Write down any **obvious** points.

   (e) Sketch the curve. (Do **not** plot!)

4 Use the methods developed so far to sketch the curve:

$$x = \frac{2t}{1 - t}, \quad y = \frac{t^2}{1 - t}$$

In particular you should find any asymptotes and examine what happens as $t \to \pm\infty$.

Trigonometric ratios

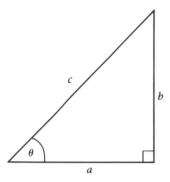

You know that:

$$\sin \theta = \frac{b}{c}$$

$$\cos \theta = \frac{a}{c}$$

$$\tan \theta = \frac{b}{a}$$

There are three other trigonometric ratios which are sometimes used. They are secant (usually abbreviated to sec), cosecant (cosec) and cotangent (cot).

In the triangle above:

$\sec \theta$ is $\dfrac{c}{a}$

$\csc \theta$ is $\dfrac{c}{b}$

$\cot \theta$ is $\dfrac{a}{b}$

1   Show that:

(a) $\sec \theta = \dfrac{1}{\cos \theta}$ (b) $\csc \theta = \dfrac{1}{\sin \theta}$

(c) $\cot \theta = \dfrac{1}{\tan \theta}$ (d) $\cot \theta = \dfrac{\cos \theta}{\sin \theta}$

2   The diagram shows the graph of $\cos \theta$
for $0 \leqslant \theta \leqslant 2\pi$ and part of the

graph of $\sec \theta = \dfrac{1}{\cos \theta}$.

Copy the diagram and complete the graph
of $\sec \theta$.

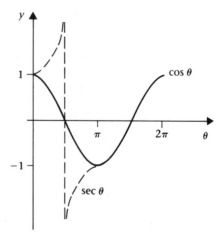

3 (a) Sketch on one diagram the graphs of sin θ and cosec θ.

   (b) Sketch on one diagram the graphs of tan θ and cot θ.

4 There is a good reason for the names of the trigonometric ratios being as they are. For $0 \leqslant \theta \leqslant \frac{1}{2}\pi$, the gradient of the graph of cos θ is negative. For which other two graphs is this the case?

   What do you notice about the names of the three ratios whose graphs have a negative gradient for $0 \leqslant \theta \leqslant \frac{1}{2}\pi$?

5 You know that, for any value of θ:

$$\sin^2\theta + \cos^2\theta = 1 \qquad ①$$

   (a) By dividing each term of equation ① by $\cos^2\theta$, show that:

$$\tan^2\theta + 1 = \sec^2\theta \qquad ②$$

   (b) By dividing each term of equation ① by $\sin^2\theta$, show that:

$$1 + \cot^2\theta = \mathrm{cosec}^2\theta \qquad ③$$

If $x = 2 \sec \theta$ and $y = 3 \tan \theta$, identity ② above can be used to write x in terms of y:

$$\sec \theta = \frac{x}{2} \quad \text{and} \quad \tan \theta = \frac{y}{3}$$

Substituting in ②,

$$\left(\frac{y}{3}\right)^2 + 1 = \left(\frac{x}{2}\right)^2$$

$$\Rightarrow \frac{y^2}{9} + 1 = \frac{x^2}{4}$$

$$\Rightarrow 4y^2 + 36 = 9x^2$$

6 Use identity ③ to convert the parametric equations:

$$x = \cot \theta \quad \text{and} \quad 2y = \mathrm{cosec}\, \theta$$

   into the Cartesian equation.

2 Product rule

2.1 Combined functions

It is always possible to estimate numerically the gradient at any point of a locally straight curve and you also know how to work out the gradients of many such curves algebraically.

The diagrams below show three curves with their tangents at $x = 1$, $x = 1.5$ and $x = 2$ respectively.

In two cases you should be able to work out an algebraic expression for $\dfrac{dy}{dx}$ and so find the equation of the tangent. In the other case you will only be able to find the gradient of the tangent by a numerical method.

In which case must you use a numerical method? Think of some other functions for which you do not yet know how to work out a derivative. What sorts of function are they?

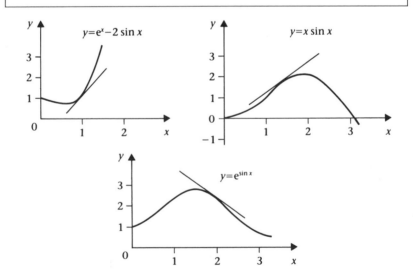

You know how to deal with functions of functions (like $\sin x^2$) by using the chain rule.

You also know that, to differentiate compound functions which have been obtained by addition or subtraction (like $x^2 - \sin x$), you merely add or subtract the separate derivatives.

It is unfortunate that derivatives of products (like $x \sin x$) cannot be dealt with by multiplying the separate derivatives.

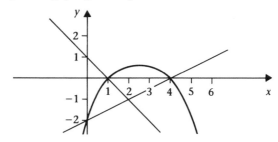

The diagram shows the graphs of the two linear functions $y = 1 - x$ and $y = \frac{1}{2}x - 2$, together with the graph of their product, $y = (1 - x)(\frac{1}{2}x - 2)$. It is clear that the two linear graphs have gradients -1 and $\frac{1}{2}$ respectively for any value of x. However, the gradient of the product graph is changing and so cannot have the value $-1 \times \frac{1}{2} = -\frac{1}{2}$ for every value of x.

You could, of course, differentiate the product function by first multiplying out the brackets, but this method will be lengthy for functions like $(2 + 3x)^2(3 - 2x)^3$ and it is not possible to 'multiply out' a product like $x \sin x$. It would therefore be very useful to find a formula for the derivative of a product.

E X A M P L E   1

Let $y = uv$, where $u = ax + b$ and $v = cx + d$.
Work out $\dfrac{dy}{dx}$ and show that it is equal to $u\dfrac{dv}{dx} + v\dfrac{du}{dx}$.

S O L U T I O N

$$y = (ax + b)(cx + d) = acx^2 + adx + bcx + bd$$

$$\frac{dy}{dx} = 2acx + ad + bc$$

$$u\frac{dv}{dx} + v\frac{du}{dx} = (ax + b)c + (cx + d)a = 2acx + ad + bc$$

Check the formula $\dfrac{dy}{dx} = u\dfrac{dv}{dx} + v\dfrac{du}{dx}$ when $u = 1 - x$
and $v = \frac{1}{2}x - 2$.

23

2.2 The product rule

You have just seen that, for a function $y = uv$, where u and v are linear functions of x:

$$\frac{dy}{dx} = v \frac{du}{dx} + u \frac{dv}{dx}$$

This rule is called the **product rule**. It would be of limited use if it could only be used for linear functions. This section considers its use for other functions.

A function which is differentiable has a graph which is locally straight. Since the product rule can be proved to be true for linear functions, you would expect the rule to be true for **any** two differentiable functions.

TASKSHEET 1 — Products (page 36)

You have seen some evidence for the following result:

The product rule holds for general functions u and v.

$$\frac{d}{dx}(uv) = u \frac{dv}{dx} + v \frac{du}{dx}$$

EXERCISE 1

1 Use the product rule to work out the derivatives of:

(a) $e^x \sin x$ (b) $x^2 e^x$ (c) $x^3 \cos x$

2 Work out the gradients of:

(a) the tangent to $y = x^3 e^x$ at $x = 2$;   (b) the tangent to $y = 2x^2 e^x$ at $x = 1$.

3 Use the product rule to differentiate $x \sin x$ and hence work out the equation of the tangent shown in the second diagram at the start of this chapter. (Work to 2 s.f.)

4 A rectangle on a computer screen has width, w, height, h, and area, A. w and h are programmed to be functions of time, t.

(a) (i) If $w = t^2$ and $h = \sin t$, use the product rule to find $\dfrac{dA}{dt}$ and so work out the rate at which the area of the rectangle is increasing when $t = 1$.

(ii) What is happening to the area when $t = 2.5$?

(b) (i) If $w = \sin t$ and $h = \cos t$, how fast is the area increasing when $t = 0.5$?

(ii) At what value of t does the area of this rectangle first stop increasing?

5 Differentiate $0.25xe^x$ and so find the equation of the tangent. (Work to 2 d.p.)

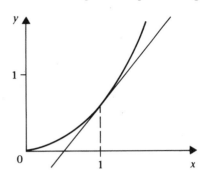

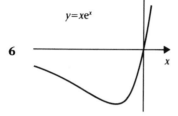

$y = xe^x$

6 Differentiate xe^x and so work out the coordinates of the turning point on the graph of $y = xe^x$.

7E (a) Differentiate x^2e^x and explain how this shows that the graph of $y = x^2e^x$ must have a stationary point at $(0, 0)$.

(b) How do you know that there is only one other stationary point on the graph? Work out the coordinates of this stationary point.

8E (a) Let $y = uv$, where $u = x$ and $v = \dfrac{1}{x}$.

It follows that $y = x \times \dfrac{1}{x} = 1$ and $\dfrac{dy}{dx} = 0$.

But $\dfrac{dy}{dx} = v\,\dfrac{du}{dx} + u\,\dfrac{dv}{dx}$

Use the above to find $\dfrac{dv}{dx}$. Hence show that the derivative of $\dfrac{1}{x}$ is $-\dfrac{1}{x^2}$.

(b) Show that the answer $\dfrac{dv}{dx} = -\dfrac{1}{x^2}$ agrees with the one obtained by using the nx^{n-1} rule.

9E Show that there is a stationary point on the curve $y = x \sin x$ when $x + \tan x = 0$. Show graphically that $x + \tan x = 0$ has three solutions in the region $-3 \leqslant x \leqslant 3$.

One of these three solutions should be obvious. Use any method you wish to find the other two solutions and so work out the coordinates of the stationary points of $y = x \sin x$ in the region $-3 \leqslant x \leqslant 3$.

2.3 Product rule and chain rule

It is very important to be clear when you need to use the chain rule and when you need to use the product rule.

$e^x \sin x$ means $e^x \times \sin x$, so two simple functions are being multiplied together and the product rule is needed.

$e^{\sin x}$ is a composite function $fg(x)$ where $g(x) = \sin x$ and $f(x) = e^x$, so the chain rule is needed.

It is sometimes necessary to use both rules.

EXAMPLE 2

Find $\dfrac{dy}{dx}$ where $y = e^{2x} \sin 0.5x$.

SOLUTION

$y = uv$, where:

$$u = e^{2x} \quad \text{and} \quad v = \sin 0.5x$$

By the chain rule, $\dfrac{du}{dx} = 2e^{2x}$ and $\dfrac{dv}{dx} = 0.5 \cos 0.5x$

By the product rule, $\dfrac{dy}{dx} = v \dfrac{du}{dx} + u \dfrac{dv}{dx}$

So $\dfrac{dy}{dx} = \sin 0.5x \times 2e^{2x} + e^{2x} \times 0.5 \cos 0.5x$

Or $\dfrac{dy}{dx} = e^{2x}(2 \sin 0.5x + 0.5 \cos 0.5x)$

EXERCISE 2

1 Differentiate these products, using both the chain rule and the product rule. Set out your working as in example 2.

(a) $2e^{3x} \sin 2x$

(b) $e^{2x} \cos 3x$

(c) $e^{x^2} \sin 4x$

2 For each part of this question, state whether you will need to use the product rule or the chain rule or both in order to differentiate the function.

(a) $\ln(x^2 + 1)$ (b) $x \ln x$ (c) $x \sin^2 x$

(d) $x \sin x^2$ (e) $(x + \sin x)^2$ (f) $e^x \cos x + x \sin x$

(g) $(2x + 3)^{-1}$ (h) $x^2 e^{3x}$

3 Differentiate each of the functions in question 2.

4 Work out the gradient of each graph at $x = 2$.

(a)

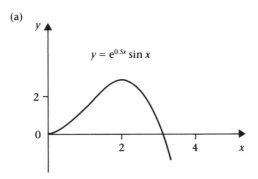

$y = e^{0.5x} \sin x$

(b)

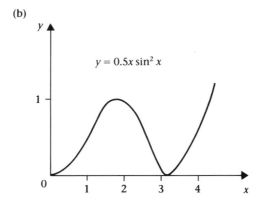

$y = 0.5x \sin^2 x$

5 The tip of a tuning fork moves so that its distance in centimetres from a central position is given by:

$$s = 0.4 \sin 512\pi t, \quad \text{where } t \text{ is the time in seconds}$$

(a) What are the displacement and the velocity of the tip of the tuning fork after 1 second?

(b) How many vibrations per second does the fork make?

6 Differentiate $\dfrac{x + 2}{x + 1}$ by writing the function as $(x + 2)(x + 1)^{-1}$.

2.4 Differentiating quotients

When tackling exercise 2, you probably found the

derivative of $\dfrac{(x + 2)}{(x + 1)}$ to be:

$$(x + 1)^{-1} + -1(x + 1)^{-2}(x + 2)$$

You may have rearranged the answer as $\dfrac{1}{x + 1} - \dfrac{x + 2}{(x + 1)^2}$.

This is still not a very neat answer, and it can be simplified further:

$$\frac{(x + 1) - (x + 2)}{(x + 1)^2} = \frac{-1}{(x + 1)^2}$$

It is possible to differentiate any quotient by rewriting the function with negative indices and using the product rule, but the process of writing the answer in a neat form is tedious. It is therefore worthwhile to try to find a formula for the derivative of a quotient.

T A S K S H E E T 2 – Quotients (page 37)

The quotient rule

If $y = \dfrac{u}{v}$, where u and v are functions of x,

then $\dfrac{dy}{dx} = \dfrac{v\dfrac{du}{dx} - u\dfrac{dv}{dx}}{v^2}$.

E X A M P L E 3

Use the quotient rule to differentiate $\dfrac{x^2}{(2x + 3)}$.

S O L U T I O N

$$y = \frac{u}{v}, \quad \text{where } u = x^2 \quad \text{and} \quad v = 2x + 3$$

$$\frac{dy}{dx} = \frac{v\dfrac{du}{dx} - u\dfrac{dv}{dx}}{v^2} = \frac{2x(2x + 3) - 2x^2}{(2x + 3)^2} = \frac{2x^2 + 6x}{(2x + 3)^2}$$

(a) Explain why $y = \dfrac{x^2}{2x + 3}$ has stationary points at $x = 0$ and $x = -3$.

(b) Evaluate the y-coordinates of the stationary points and explain why $x = -3$ gives a local maximum.

EXERCISE 3

1   Differentiate: (a) $\dfrac{\sin x}{x}$ (b) $\dfrac{x}{e^x}$ (c) $\dfrac{e^x}{\sin x}$ (d) $\dfrac{e^{3x}}{\sin 2x}$

2   Work out the gradients of:

(a) $y = \dfrac{\sin x}{e^x}$ at $x = -1$ (b) $y = \dfrac{e^{2x}}{x^2}$ at $x = 0.8$

Use a graph plotter to check that your answers look reasonable.

3   You can differentiate $\dfrac{1}{(2x + 3)} = (2x + 3)^{-1}$ by using either the quotient rule or the chain rule. Work out the derivative using each method in turn. Which method do you prefer?

4   (a) The graph of $y = \dfrac{x}{1 + x^2}$ has a local minimum and a local maximum.
    Work out the coordinates of these points, showing clearly how you know which is the maximum and which is the minimum.

(b) Repeat (a) for $y = \dfrac{x^2}{x + 4}$.

5   Use the quotient rule to differentiate $\tan x = \dfrac{\sin x}{\cos x}$.

6   Work out the derivative of $\cot x$ by writing:

(a) $\cot x = \dfrac{\cos x}{\sin x}$;   (b) $\cot x = \dfrac{1}{\tan x}$.

(c) Check that your answers to parts (a) and (b) are consistent by writing each one in as simple a form as you can.

7E   The first part of an alternative proof of the quotient rule, assuming that the product rule is true, is given below. Try to complete the proof.

$y = \dfrac{u}{v}$ where u and v are functions of x. Then $u = vy$.

By the product rule, $\dfrac{du}{dx} = \ldots$

2.5 Implicit differentiation

You know how to differentiate functions of functions, sums, differences, products and quotients of functions.

However, all the functions which you have been asked to differentiate have been stated **explicitly**, i.e. as $y = f(x)$.

However, functions are sometimes stated **implicitly**. For example, the equation of the circle, centre $(0, 0)$ and radius 3 units, is usually given in the implicit form:

$$x^2 + y^2 = 9$$

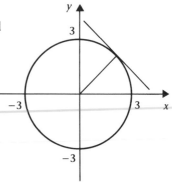

You can find $\dfrac{dy}{dx}$ from this implicit equation by finding the derivative of both sides of the equation, with respect to x.

$$\frac{d}{dx}(x^2) + \frac{d}{dx}(y^2) = \frac{d}{dx}(9)$$

You can easily work out two of the three derivatives above, since you know that $\dfrac{d}{dx}(x^2) = 2x$ and $\dfrac{d}{dx}(9) = 0$.

(a) Let $z = y^2$. Use the chain rule, $\dfrac{dz}{dx} = \dfrac{dz}{dy} \times \dfrac{dy}{dx}$, to show that $\dfrac{d}{dx}(y^2) = 2y\dfrac{dy}{dx}$.

(b) Hence show that $\dfrac{dy}{dx} = -\dfrac{x}{y}$.

(c) Explain how the answer to (b) gives the expected values for the gradients of the tangents to the circle at the points $(0, 3)$, $(3, 0)$, $(0, -3)$ and $(-3, 0)$.

The process used in the discussion point is called **implicit differentiation**.

EXAMPLE 4

Use implicit differentiation to find $\dfrac{dy}{dx}$ if:

$$x^3 + 3y^2 - 4x + y = 11$$

SOLUTION

$$\dfrac{d}{dx}(x^3) + \dfrac{d}{dx}(3y^2) - \dfrac{d}{dx}(4x) + \dfrac{d}{dx}(y) = \dfrac{d}{dx}(11)$$

$$3x^2 + 6y\dfrac{dy}{dx} - 4 + \dfrac{dy}{dx} = 0$$

$$\dfrac{dy}{dx}(6y + 1) + 3x^2 - 4 = 0$$

$$\dfrac{dy}{dx}(6y + 1) = 4 - 3x^2$$

$$\dfrac{dy}{dx} = \dfrac{4 - 3x^2}{6y + 1}$$

The point $(1, 2)$ lies on the graph of $x^3 + 3y^2 - 4x + y = 11$.

(a) What is the gradient of the tangent at the point $(1, 2)$?

(b) Work out the equation of this tangent.

EXERCISE 4

1 Use implicit differentiation to find $\dfrac{dy}{dx}$ when:

(a) $2y^2 - 3y + 4x^2 = 2$ (b) $x^3 + \tfrac{1}{2}y^2 - 7x + 3y = 3$

2 The graph of $9x^2 + 4y^2 = 45$ is as shown.

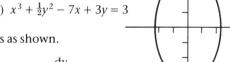

(a) Use implicit differentiation to find $\dfrac{dy}{dx}$.

(b) Work out the y-coordinates of the two points where $x = 1$ and calculate the gradients at these points.
(Check that your results look reasonable.)

31

3   The circle with centre $(-3, 1)$ and radius 5 units has equation:

$$(x + 3)^2 + (y - 1)^2 = 25$$

i.e. $x^2 + 6x + y^2 - 2y = 15$

(a) Work out an expression for $\dfrac{dy}{dx}$ and use it to find the equation of the tangent to the circle at the point $(1, 4)$.

(b) The point $(1, -2)$ lies on the circumference of the circle. Work out the gradient of the tangent at this point and the gradient of the radius of the circle to this point. Check that your results are in agreement with the property of circles that a tangent is always perpendicular to the radius at that point.

(c) Repeat (b) for any other point on the circumference of the circle.

4   You have seen that the circle $x^2 + y^2 = 9$ can be written in parametric form as:

$$x = 3 \cos \theta; \qquad y = 3 \sin \theta$$

Parametric differentiation gives the result:

$$\frac{dy}{dx} = -\frac{\cos \theta}{\sin \theta}$$

Explain why this result is equivalent to the result $\dfrac{dy}{dx} = -\dfrac{x}{y}$, which was obtained in the discussion point in this section. Also explain why the results show that the angle between tangent and radius must always be a right-angle in this circle.

5   In earlier work, you obtained the following results by numerical methods:

$$\frac{d}{dx}(2^x) = 0.693 \times 2^x$$

$$\frac{d}{dx}(3^x) = 1.10 \times 3^x$$

You can now obtain these results using implicit differentiation and the fact that:

$$y = 2^x$$
$$\Rightarrow \ln y = \ln 2^x$$
$$\Rightarrow \ln y = x \ln 2$$

(a) Explain why $\dfrac{d}{dx}(\ln y) = \dfrac{1}{y}\dfrac{dy}{dx}$ and hence find $\dfrac{dy}{dx}$ (i.e. the derivative of 2^x). Show that your answer agrees with the numerical result.

(b) Work out the derivative of 3^x using implicit differentiation.

(c) What is the derivative of a^x, where a is any constant?

2.6 Implicit differentiation and the product rule

The equation considered in the previous section:

$$x^2 + y^2 = 9$$

could have been rewritten as:

$$y = \pm \sqrt{(9 - x^2)}$$

and differentiated in the usual way. However, implicit differentiation is much easier. In some cases, just rewriting an equation in the form $y = f(x)$ is itself very difficult or even impossible.

E X A M P L E 5

Find $\dfrac{dy}{dx}$ when $y^2 + xy + x^2 = 8$.

S O L U T I O N

Consider the xy term first.

Let $z = xy$ and use the product rule with $u = x$ and $v = y$.

Then $\dfrac{du}{dx} = 1$ and $\dfrac{dv}{dx} = \dfrac{dy}{dx}$

$$\dfrac{dz}{dx} = v \dfrac{du}{dx} + u \dfrac{dv}{dx}$$

$$= y \times 1 + x \times \dfrac{dy}{dx}$$

$$= y + x \dfrac{dy}{dx}$$

Now differentiate each term of the original expression.

$$y^2 + \quad xy \quad + x^2 = 8$$

$$\Rightarrow 2y \dfrac{dy}{dx} + \left(y + x \dfrac{dy}{dx} \right) + 2x = 0$$

Then $(2y + x)\dfrac{dy}{dx} + y + 2x = 0$

$$\Rightarrow \dfrac{dy}{dx}(2y + x) = -(y + 2x)$$

$$\Rightarrow \dfrac{dy}{dx} = \dfrac{-(y + 2x)}{(2y + x)}$$

33

EXERCISE 5

1 Work out $\dfrac{dy}{dx}$ for:

(a) $2x^2 + 3xy - 4y + y^2 = 5$

(b) $y^2 - 2xy + 3x - x^2 = 1$

(c) $x^2 + 4y^2 - 4x + 8y = 28$

(d) $y^3 + x^3 + xy^2 = 4$

2 For $xy = 12$:

(a) differentiate implicitly to find $\dfrac{dy}{dx}$;

(b) express y as an explicit function of x and differentiate to find $\dfrac{dy}{dx}$;

(c) show that your answers to (a) and (b) are the same.

3 (a) Check that the point $(-2, 3)$ is on the graph of:

$$x^2y + x^3 = 4$$

(b) Use implicit differentiation to find $\dfrac{dy}{dx}$ and so show that $(-2, 3)$ is a stationary point on the curve.

(c) Show that $x^2y + x^3 = 4$ can be rewritten as:

$$y = \frac{4 - x^3}{x^2}$$

(d) Use the quotient rule to find $\dfrac{dy}{dx}$ and show that this also indicates a stationary point at $x = -2$.

4 (a) Find $\dfrac{dy}{dx}$ if $3xy - 2x^2 = 8$ and so show that the graph of $3xy - 2x^2 = 8$ has stationary points at $(2, 2\frac{2}{3})$ and $(-2, -2\frac{2}{3})$.

(b) Rewrite $3xy - 2x^2 = 8$ in the form $y = f(x)$ and use the quotient rule to check the coordinates of the stationary points.

(c) Do you prefer implicit differentiation or rearrangement and use of the quotient rule for checking the coordinates of stationary points? Which would you use if you had to **find** the coordinates of stationary points?

 TASKSHEET 3S — Differentiation practice (page 38)

After working through this chapter you should:

1 know how to differentiate products and quotients using the two rules:

- Product rule:

$$\frac{d}{dx}(uv) = v\,\frac{du}{dx} + u\,\frac{dv}{dx}$$

- Quotient rule:

$$\frac{d}{dx}\left(\frac{u}{v}\right) = \frac{v\,\dfrac{du}{dx} - u\,\dfrac{dv}{dx}}{v^2}$$

2 understand the importance of approaching differentiation systematically and recognise when to use the chain rule and when to use the product rule;

3 know how to use implicit differentiation and be aware that this will involve the use of the chain rule and sometimes also the product rule.

Products

1

This tasksheet provides some evidence that the product rule works for any two differentiable functions.

1

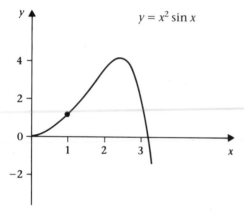

$y = x^2 \sin x$

(a) Use the product rule to find the gradient of $y = x^2 \sin x$ at $x = 1$ and check that your answer seems reasonable in view of the shape of the graph of $y = x^2 \sin x$.

(b) Use a numerical method to evaluate the gradient of $y = x^2 \sin x$ at $x = 1$ and check that it agrees with your answer to (a).

2 (a) Use the product rule to obtain the equation of the gradient graph for $y = uv$ where $u = \cos \frac{1}{2}x$ and $v = 4x - \frac{1}{2}x^2$.

(b) Use a program for numerical gradients to check your answer to (a).

3 Repeat question 2 for any two functions you choose.

4 (a) x^5 can be written as $x^3 \times x^2$.

Use the product rule with $u = x^3$ and $v = x^2$ and check that you do obtain the derivative of x^5.

(b) Write x^8 as a product in at least two different ways. In each case, differentiate using the product rule and check that you obtain $8x^7$.

(c) $x^{a+b} = x^a \times x^b$

Differentiate $x^a \times x^b$ using the product rule. Do you obtain the expected answer?

Quotients

1 $y = \dfrac{x}{\sin x} = x(\sin x)^{-1}$

Show that $\dfrac{dy}{dx} = \dfrac{\sin x - x \cos x}{\sin^2 x}$

Alternatively, $\dfrac{x}{\sin x}$ can be differentiated by considering it as $\dfrac{u}{v}$ instead of as uv.

$$u = x, \quad v = \sin x, \quad \frac{du}{dx} = 1 \quad \text{and} \quad \frac{dv}{dx} = \cos x$$

·

So $\dfrac{dy}{dx} = \dfrac{v\dfrac{du}{dx} - u\dfrac{dv}{dx}}{v^2}$ ①

2 (a) Differentiate $\dfrac{e^x}{\sin x}$ by writing the function as $e^x(\sin x)^{-1}$.

Check whether the answer agrees with the one you would obtain by using formula ①.

(b) Repeat part (a) for any quotient of your choice.

3 Formula ① is called the **quotient rule** and it is true for any quotient $\dfrac{u}{v}$, where u

and v are differentiable functions of x. Here is the start of a proof of the rule.

$$y = \frac{u}{v} = uv^{-1}$$

So, by the product rule:

$$\frac{dy}{dx} = v^{-1}\frac{du}{dx} + u\frac{d(v^{-1})}{dx}$$

Use the chain rule to work out $\dfrac{d(v^{-1})}{dx}$ and so complete the proof.

Differentiation practice

3S

Work through this tasksheet if you feel that you need more practice at differentiation techniques and choosing which technique to use. You will need to use the chain rule, product rule and quotient rule, as well as parametric and implicit differentiation.

Find $\dfrac{dy}{dx}$ when:

1 $y = \sin^2 x$

2 $y = 3 \cos 4x$

3 $y = \dfrac{1}{x^2}$

4 $y = \dfrac{1}{2x + 5}$

5 $x = t^2; \quad y = 3(2t + 1)$

6 $y = e^{2x} \sin \frac{1}{2}x$

7 $y = (2x^2 - 3)^3$

8 $y = \ln 4x$

9 $x^2 y = 36$

10 $x = 4 \cos \theta; \quad y = 3 \sin \theta$

11 $y = x(2x - 3)^4$

12 $y = x^4(2x - 3)$

13 $x = \sin 2\theta; \quad y = 2 \cos 3\theta$

14 $x^2 + y^2 = 25$

15 $y = \sqrt{(5x)}$

16 $x = \dfrac{1}{t}; \quad y = t^3$

17 $x^2 + 3xy + 2y^2 = 8$

18 $y = \dfrac{\sin x}{\cos 2x}$

19 $e^{3x} y = x^2$

20 $x^2 + y = 12$

3 Volume

3.1 Containers

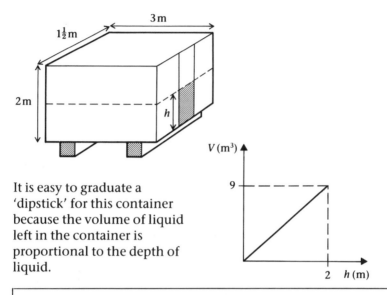

It is easy to graduate a 'dipstick' for this container because the volume of liquid left in the container is proportional to the depth of liquid.

Not all industrial containers are quite so simple. Calculate the volume of each of these containers and make a rough sketch of what you think the (h, V) graph will look like.

(a)

(b)

(c) $y = x^2$

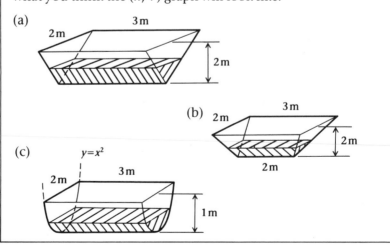

TASKSHEET 1 — Thin slabs (page 47)

One technique often used to calculate the volume of a solid is to imagine the solid as a large number of thin slabs. If the horizontal cross-sectional area can be expressed as a function of the vertical height, then the volume of the solid can be calculated.

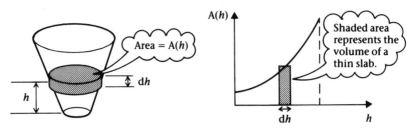

If $A(h)$ is the cross-sectional area of a solid at height h then the volume is given by:

$$V = \int A(h)\, dh$$

E X A M P L E 1

A container and a horizontal cross-section are shown below.

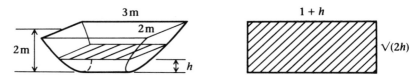

The depth of liquid increases from $h = 0.6\,\text{m}$ to $h = 1.2\,\text{m}$. Calculate the increase in volume.

S O L U T I O N

The horizontal cross-sectional area at depth h is
$(1 + h)\sqrt{(2h)} = \sqrt{2}(h^{0.5} + h^{1.5})\,\text{m}^2$.

$$\int_{0.6}^{1.2} (1 + h)\sqrt{(2h)}\, dh = \sqrt{2} \int_{0.6}^{1.2} h^{0.5} + h^{1.5}\, dh$$

$$= \sqrt{2} \left[\tfrac{2}{3}h^{1.5} + \tfrac{2}{5}h^{2.5} \right]_{0.6}^{1.2}$$

$$= 1.536\,\text{m}^3 \quad \text{(or 1536 litres)}$$

Calculate the volume of the container when full.

3.2 Volumes of revolution

A solid with the same shape as a wine glass can be produced by spinning the area between the graph of $y = x^2$, the line $y = 4$ and the y-axis about the y-axis.

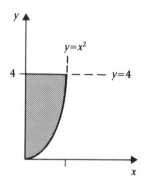

The horizontal cross-sectional areas you would use to calculate the volume of the glass are particularly simple, as they are all circles. Solids formed in such a way are called **solids of revolution**.

Solids can also be formed by rotating an area about an axis. Sketch the solid formed by rotating the area between the graph of $y = x^2$, the line $x = 2$ and the x-axis about the x-axis.

TASKSHEET 2 – *Volumes (page 49)*

The two shaded areas shown on the graph are equal.

Would you expect the volume generated by rotating area A about the x-axis to be the same as that obtained by rotating B about the y-axis?

Justify your answer.

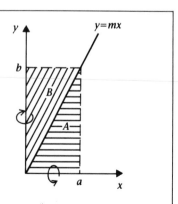

> If the area between $y = f(x)$ and the x-axis for $a < x < b$ is rotated about the x-axis, then the solid formed will have volume:
>
> $$V = \pi \int_a^b y^2 \, dx$$
>
> Similarly, if the area between $y = f(x)$ and the y-axis for $c < y < d$ is rotated about the y-axis, then the solid formed will have volume:
>
> $$V = \pi \int_c^d x^2 \, dy$$

EXAMPLE 2

The shaded area shown is part of a circle with centre at the origin and radius r.

Rotate this area about the x-axis and hence prove that the volume of a sphere is given by the formula:

$$V = \tfrac{4}{3}\pi r^3$$

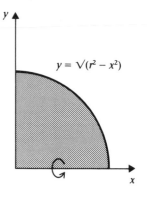

$y = \sqrt{(r^2 - x^2)}$

SOLUTION

The solid generated will be a hemisphere and its volume is:

$$V = \pi \int_0^r y^2 \, dx$$

But $y^2 = r^2 - x^2$

$$\Rightarrow V = \pi \int_0^r r^2 - x^2 \, dx$$

$$= \pi \left[r^2 x - \tfrac{1}{3}x^3 \right]_0^r$$

$$= \tfrac{2}{3}\pi r^3$$

The volume of a sphere is twice the volume of a hemisphere and so the formula is proved.

3.3 Integration by inspection

You have now used integration to find areas and volumes and to solve differential equations. You also know that to integrate a function you only need to find a function whose derivative is the original function. Unfortunately, this is far from simple in practice, as many functions **cannot** be integrated algebraically. Definite integrals can always be evaluated numerically, but having an algebraic solution is often more convenient and may even be essential in obtaining a complete solution to a problem. When integrating, it is important to know how to choose the best method.

E X A M P L E 3

Find $\int \sin 3x - x^2 \, dx$.

S O L U T I O N

Always try to integrate by inspection first, since this is likely to give the answer more quickly.

$$\int \sin 3x - x^2 \, dx = -\tfrac{1}{3} \cos 3x - \tfrac{1}{3}x^3 + c$$

E X A M P L E 4

Find $\int (x^5 - 3x^2)(4x^3 - 3) \, dx$.

S O L U T I O N

In some cases it is necessary to multiply out brackets first.

$$\int (x^5 - 3x^2)(4x^3 - 3) \, dx = \int 4x^8 - 15x^5 + 9x^2 \, dx = \tfrac{4}{9}x^9 - \tfrac{15}{6}x^6 + 3x^3 + c$$

To integrate a function by inspection, you must first think of a function which is likely to differentiate to the original function. You then compare the derived function with the function you want and make any small adjustment as necessary.

E X A M P L E 5

Find $\int xe^{3x^2} \, dx$.

S O L U T I O N

Differentiating the function e^{3x^2} seems to be a sensible starting point.

$$\frac{d}{dx}(e^{3x^2}) = 6x\,e^{3x^2} \implies \frac{d}{dx}(\tfrac{1}{6}e^{3x^2}) = x\,e^{3x^2}$$

$$\implies \int x\,e^{3x^2}\,dx = \tfrac{1}{6}e^{3x^2} + c$$

> Discuss what functions you might try to differentiate to solve the following integrals.
>
> (a) $\displaystyle\int x\cos x^2\,dx$ (b) $\displaystyle\int x\cos 2x\,dx$
>
> (c) $\displaystyle\int \cos 2x\,dx$ (d) $\displaystyle\int \cos x^2\,dx$

The discussion point illustrates the difficulty of integration compared with differentiation. In (a) and (b) the function being integrated is the product of two functions. (a) looks more complicated, but proves to be an easy 'backward' chain rule, while (b) requires the product rule and some very clear thinking. (c) and (d) both look straightforward, but (d) cannot be integrated algebraically.

EXERCISE 1

1   Find   (a) $\displaystyle\int \cos 3x\,dx$ (b) $\displaystyle\int (x+2)(x-2)\,dx$

(c) $\displaystyle\int e^{5x}\,dx$ (d) $\displaystyle\int \frac{1}{x}\,dx$

2   Write down the derivatives of:

(a) $\sin x^3$ (b) $\cos 2x^2$ (c) $(x^2 - 3)^3$

3   Use your answers to question 2 to write down the integrals of:

(a) $x^2 \cos x^3$ (b) $x \sin 2x^2$ (c) $x(x^2 - 3)^2$

4   The nose-cone of a rocket is obtained by rotating the area between the graph of $y = 3(1 - x^2)$ and the axes about the y-axis.

(a)   Draw a sketch showing the area being rotated.

(b)   Calculate the volume of the nose-cone.

5   (a)   Sketch the parabolas $y^2 = 4x$ and $y^2 = 5x - 4$ on the same axes and find their points of intersection.

(b)   A bowl is made by rotating the area enclosed by the curves about the x-axis. Find the volume of the material used to make the bowl.

3.4 Integrating trigonometric functions

You have seen that not all functions can be integrated algebraically. However, many functions which may look impossible to integrate **can** be integrated if they are first rewritten. The trigonometric identities developed in *Mathematical methods* are particularly useful.

EXAMPLE 6

Find $\int \cos^2 x \, dx$

SOLUTION

The identity $2 \cos^2 x - 1 = \cos 2x$ can be written as $\cos^2 x = \frac{1}{2} + \frac{1}{2} \cos 2x$

$$\Rightarrow \int \cos^2 x \, dx = \int \frac{1}{2} + \frac{1}{2} \cos 2x \, dx$$

$$= \tfrac{1}{2}x + \tfrac{1}{4} \sin 2x + c$$

The following identities are the **addition formulas**.

$\sin (A + B) = \sin A \cos B + \cos A \sin B$
$\sin (A - B) = \sin A \cos B - \cos A \sin B$
$\cos (A + B) = \cos A \cos B - \sin A \sin B$
$\cos (A - B) = \cos A \cos B + \sin A \sin B$

(a) Use the addition formulas to show that $\sin (\tfrac{1}{2}\pi - \theta) = \cos \theta$. Obtain similar results for $\cos (\tfrac{1}{2}\pi - \theta)$, $\sec (\tfrac{1}{2}\pi - \theta)$ and $\tan (\tfrac{1}{2}\pi - \theta)$.

(b) Show how you can use the addition formulas to prove the **sum and difference formulas.**

$2 \cos A \cos B = \cos (A + B) + \cos (A - B)$
$2 \sin A \sin B = -\cos (A + B) + \cos (A - B)$
$2 \sin A \cos B = \sin (A + B) + \sin (A - B)$

Use the sum and difference formulas to prove that:

(a) $2 \cos^2 x = 1 + \cos 2x$

(b) $2 \sin^2 x = 1 - \cos 2x$

(c) $2 \sin x \cos x = \sin 2x$

EXAMPLE 7

Find $\displaystyle\int \sin 5x \cos 2x \, dx$

SOLUTION

Using the identity $2 \sin A \cos B = \sin (A + B) + \sin (A - B)$,

$$\int \sin 5x \cos 2x \, dx = \int \tfrac{1}{2} \sin 7x + \tfrac{1}{2} \sin 3x \, dx$$
$$= -\tfrac{1}{14} \cos 7x - \tfrac{1}{6} \cos 3x + c$$

EXERCISE 2

1 Find (a) $\displaystyle\int \sin x \cos x \, dx$ (b) $\displaystyle\int \sin 3x \cos 3x \, dx$

2 Find (a) $\displaystyle\int \cos 5x \cos x \, dx$ (b) $\displaystyle\int \sin 3x \sin 7x \, dx$

3 Find $\displaystyle\int_0^{\frac{1}{4}\pi} \cos^2 x \, dx$

4 Calculate the volume generated by rotating the shaded area about the x-axis.

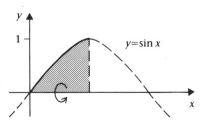

After working through this chapter you should:

1 know how to use integration to calculate a volume by

- integrating a cross-sectional area with respect to height,

$$V = \int A(h) \, dh;$$

- rotating an area about the x-axis, $V = \pi \displaystyle\int y^2 \, dx;$

- rotating an area about the y-axis, $V = \pi \displaystyle\int x^2 \, dy;$

2 know how to integrate a function by inspection;

3 know how to use trigonometric identities to rewrite an expression so that it can be integrated by inspection.

Thin slabs

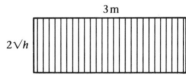

One way to solve the problem of graduating a dipstick for the container illustrated above is to consider it as a number of thin horizontal slabs, each of thickness dh.

The width of a slab at distance h
from the bottom will be $2\sqrt{h}$, . . .

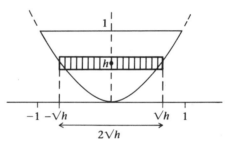

the horizontal cross-sectional
area will be $6\sqrt{h}$, . . .

and the volume of the
slab will therefore be $6\sqrt{h}\,dh$.

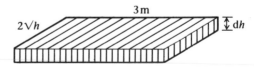

The total volume of the container will be the sum of the volumes of the thin slabs.

$$V = \int_0^1 6\sqrt{h}\,dh \qquad \text{NB } \sqrt{h} = h^{0.5}$$

$$= \left[4h^{1.5} \right]_0^1$$

$$= 4\,\text{m}^3 \quad \text{(or 4000 litres)}$$

47

The (h, V) graph for the container is as shown.

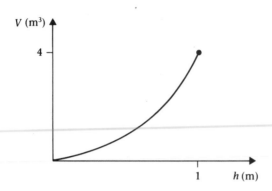

1   At what depth will the container be:

(a) a quarter full,   (b) half full,   (c) three-quarters full?

Another container is shown below.

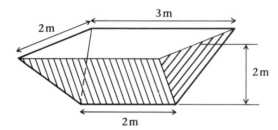

2   Explain why a thin slab at height h will have the dimensions shown below.

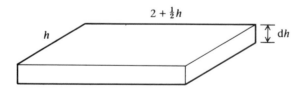

3   Calculate the volume of the container and sketch the (h, V) graph.

4   For what value of h is the container half full?

5   The depth of liquid in the container increases from 1.1 m to 1.4 m. What is the increase in volume?

Volumes

1 The graph of $y = x^2$ for $0 \leqslant x \leqslant 2$ is rotated about the x-axis.

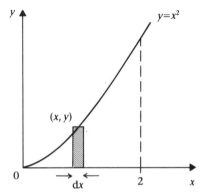

(a) Explain why the volume obtained by rotating the shaded strip is approximately $\pi y^2 \, dx$.

(b) If you consider the area as being made up of a large number of thin strips of this kind, the volume is:

$$\int_0^2 \pi y^2 \, dx$$

To be able to integrate this you must write y^2 in terms of x. What will this give?

(c) Evaluate the volume.

2 Work out the volumes obtained by rotating each of these shaded areas about the x-axis.

(a)

(b)

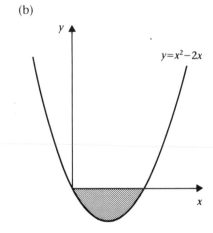

3 Work out the volume obtained by rotating $y = x^2$ for $0 \leqslant y \leqslant 4$ about the **y-axis**.

Work as in question 1 by first writing down the volume obtained by rotating the shaded strip about the y-axis.

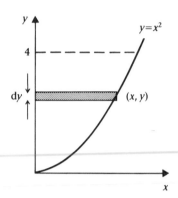

4 Work out the volume obtained by rotating the area bounded by the curve $y = \dfrac{1}{x}$, the y-axis and the lines $y = 1$ and $y = 2$ about the y-axis. (First draw a sketch to show the area being rotated.)

5 Work out the volume of the vase obtained by rotating the outline illustrated below about the y-axis. The curved section is part of a circle with centre the origin and radius 5 units.

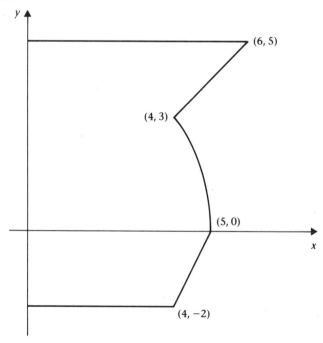

4 Integration techniques

4.1 Integration by parts

You know that not all functions can be integrated using algebraic techniques and that those that can are not always straightforward. The first technique you should try when searching for an algebraic solution is 'trial and improvement' or 'inspection'. Think of a function which looks as though it might differentiate to the function you need to integrate, then differentiate it and make adjustments as necessary (for example, multiply or divide by a constant).

This chapter looks at some standard techniques which often prove useful when 'trial and improvement' fails.

The formula for the product rule for differentiation can be rearranged into a form which is helpful when integrating certain functions.

$$\frac{d}{dx}(uv) = v\frac{du}{dx} + u\frac{dv}{dx} \Rightarrow uv = \int v\frac{du}{dx}\,dx + \int u\frac{dv}{dx}\,dx$$

$$\Rightarrow \int u\frac{dv}{dx}\,dx = uv - \int v\frac{du}{dx}\,dx$$

This is called the formula for **integration by parts**. It provides an efficient method for integrating some products of functions.

E X A M P L E   1

Find $\int x \cos 2x\,dx$

S O L U T I O N

Let $u = x$, so $\frac{du}{dx} = 1$. Let $\frac{dv}{dx} = \cos 2x$, so $v = \frac{1}{2}\sin 2x$.

$$\int x \cos 2x\,dx = \tfrac{1}{2}x \sin 2x - \int \tfrac{1}{2}\sin 2x\,dx = \tfrac{1}{2}x \sin 2x + \tfrac{1}{4}\cos 2x + c$$

Integration by parts $\int u\frac{dv}{dx}\,dx = uv - \int v\frac{du}{dx}\,dx$

Integration by parts is only applicable to functions written as the product of two functions. When using the formula, always start by deciding which part of the product should be u and which should be $\dfrac{dv}{dx}$. Then write down $\dfrac{du}{dx}$ and v. Only when you have the functions u, v, $\dfrac{du}{dx}$ and $\dfrac{dv}{dx}$ clearly written down can you be reasonably sure of substituting correctly into the formula.

(a) What happens if, in the example above, you let
$$u = \cos 2x \quad \text{and} \quad \frac{dv}{dx} = x?$$

(b) What happens if you use integration by parts to find
$$\int x \cos x^2 \, dx?$$

Integration by parts gives a method for dealing with certain types of function. However, this method will not always prove successful for functions written as the product of two functions. Experience will help you decide when this method will work. The method works for all the functions in the next exercise.

EXERCISE 1

1 Find: (a) $\displaystyle\int x \, e^x \, dx$ (b) $\displaystyle\int x \, e^{3x} \, dx$ (c) $\displaystyle\int x \, e^{ax} \, dx$

2 Find: (a) $\displaystyle\int x \cos x \, dx$ (b) $\displaystyle\int x \cos 3x \, dx$ (c) $\displaystyle\int x \cos ax \, dx$

3 Use integration by parts twice to evaluate:

(a) $\displaystyle\int x^2 \, e^x \, dx$ (b) $\displaystyle\int x^2 \sin x \, dx$

4 Work out each of these definite integrals. Sketch diagrams to show the areas you have found and check that your answers seem reasonable.

(a) $\displaystyle\int_{-1}^{0} x \sin 2x \, dx$ (b) $\displaystyle\int_{-3}^{0} 2x \, e^{0.5x} \, dx$

TASKSHEET 1E — By parts (page 60)

4.2 Integration by substitution

Another useful technique of integration can be obtained from the chain rule for differentiation.

To find $\dfrac{dy}{dx}$ if $y = \sin(3x^2 + 5)$, let $u = 3x^2 + 5$ and $y = \sin u$.

$$\Rightarrow \frac{dy}{dx} = \frac{dy}{du} \times \frac{du}{dx} = \cos u \times 6x = 6x \cos(3x^2 + 5)$$

In the chain rule, the variable u is substituted for the original variable x and then x is substituted back at the end of the answer. The same technique can be used for integrating certain types of function. Changing the variable of the integral can be done using the chain rule.

$$\frac{dy}{du} = \frac{dy}{dx} \times \frac{dx}{du} \Rightarrow y = \int \frac{dy}{dx} \times \frac{dx}{du} \, du \text{ but } y = \int \frac{dy}{dx} \, dx$$

The variable of the integral can be changed from x to u by replacing 'dx' by '$\dfrac{dx}{du}\, du$'.

EXAMPLE 2

Find $y = \displaystyle\int x \cos(3x^2 + 5) \, dx$

SOLUTION

Let $u = 3x^2 + 5 \Rightarrow \dfrac{du}{dx} = 6x$ This gives $\dfrac{dx}{du} = \dfrac{1}{6x}$

$\Rightarrow y = \displaystyle\int x \cos(3x^2 + 5)\dfrac{1}{6x}\, du$ Replacing dx by $\dfrac{dx}{du}\, du$

$\Rightarrow y = \tfrac{1}{6}\displaystyle\int \cos(3x^2 + 5)\, du$ This cannot be solved as it stands. You must express the integral entirely in terms of the new variable u.

$\Rightarrow y = \tfrac{1}{6}\displaystyle\int \cos u \, du$ and so $y = \tfrac{1}{6}\sin u + c = \tfrac{1}{6}\sin(3x^2 + 5) + c$

You may have been able to solve the integral in the previous example by inspection. While using substitution is not wrong in such a case, it is unnecessarily complicated. Substitution only works for some functions and even then it is sometimes no more than a rather slow method for finding integrals which can be found by inspection. However, there are many cases where it considerably simplifies the integral. Some of these cases are considered on tasksheet 2E.

Discuss how you would find the integral of:

(a) $x(x^2 + 3)^4$ (b) $x^3(x^2 + 3)^4$ (c) $(x^2 + 3)^4$

It is important to choose the right substitution when using this method of integration. All the integrals in the exercise below lend themselves to integration by substitution, although you may feel that some of them could be done by inspection. Remember that whatever substitution you make, your final solution must be in terms of the original variable.

EXERCISE 2

1 Evaluate the following integrals by using the suggested substitution.

(a) $\int (x + 3)^5 dx$ (let $u = x + 3$)   (b) $\int x(2x - 5)^6 dx$ (let $u = 2x - 5$)

(c) $\int x^2(x - 2)^7 dx$ (let $u = x - 2$)   (d) $\int x(x^2 - 4)^8 dx$ (let $u = x^2 - 4$)

(e) $\int x^2 \sqrt{(x^3 - 2)} dx$ (let $u = x^3 - 2$)

2 Integrate the following functions using the suggested substitutions.

(a) $\sin^2 x \cos x$ (let $u = \sin x$)   (b) $\cos^2 x \sin x$ (let $u = \cos x$)

3 Integrate the following functions using a suitable substitution.

(a) $x^2 \sqrt{(x^3 + 3)}$ (b) $x(x - 3)^5$ (c) $x\sqrt{(x - 2)}$

(d) $\cos x \sin^3 x$ (e) $\cos^5 x \sin x$ (f) $\dfrac{x}{(x + 2)^3}$

TASKSHEET 2E — *Integrating the circle (page 61)*

4.3 The reciprocal function

Any integral of the form $\int \dfrac{f'(x)}{f(x)} dx$ can be integrated algebraically.

Use the method of substitution to show that:

$$\int \frac{f'(x)}{f(x)} dx = \int \frac{1}{u} du \quad \text{if } u = f(x)$$

You know that $\dfrac{d}{dx}(\ln x) = \dfrac{1}{x}$

and that $\displaystyle\int_a^b \frac{1}{x} dx = \Big[\ln x\Big]_a^b$

$$= \ln b - \ln a$$

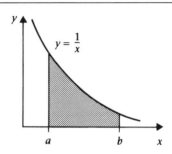

Negative values of x, however, present a problem as the function $\ln x$ is defined only for $x > 0$.

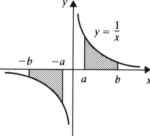

(a) Explain why $\displaystyle\int_{-b}^{-a} \frac{1}{x} dx \neq \Big[\ln x\Big]_{-b}^{-a} = \ln(-a) - \ln(-b)$

(b) By symmetry, $\displaystyle\int_{-b}^{-a} \frac{1}{x} dx = -\int_a^b \frac{1}{x} dx$. Use this to express

$\displaystyle\int_{-b}^{-a} \frac{1}{x} dx$ in terms of $\ln a$ and $\ln b$.

(c) Explain why $\displaystyle\int_{-b}^{-a} \frac{1}{x} dx = \Big[\ln|x|\Big]_{-b}^{-a}$

Why is it not possible to evaluate $\displaystyle\int_{-a}^{a} \frac{1}{x}\,dx$?

The following result forms the basis of a useful integration technique.

If the graph of f(x) is continuous between a and b then:

$$\int_a^b \frac{f'(x)}{f(x)}\,dx = \left[\, \ln|f(x)| \,\right]_a^b$$

where $|f(x)|$ denotes the absolute value of f(x).

EXAMPLE 3

Find $\displaystyle\int \frac{3}{2x-5}\,dx.$

SOLUTION

$$\int \frac{3}{2x-5}\,dx = \tfrac{3}{2}\int \frac{2}{2x-5}\,dx = \tfrac{3}{2}\ln|2x-5| + c$$

EXERCISE 3

1 Find (a) $\displaystyle\int \frac{3}{x-2}\,dx$ (b) $\displaystyle\int \frac{6}{2x+7}\,dx$ (c) $\displaystyle\int \frac{1}{3x-1}\,dx$

2 Evaluate (a) $\displaystyle\int_1^2 \frac{2}{3x-2}\,dx$ (b) $\displaystyle\int_{-2}^{-1} \frac{2}{3x-2}\,dx$

3 Explain why you cannot evaluate $\displaystyle\int_1^4 \frac{3}{x-2}\,dx.$

4 Show that:

(a) $\displaystyle\int \tan x\,dx = \ln|\sec x| + c$ (b) $\displaystyle\int \cot x\,dx = \ln|\sin x| + c$

4.4 Partial fractions

Evaluate $\displaystyle\int_1^2 \frac{5}{(x-3)(x+2)}$ dx using a numerical method

and $\displaystyle\int_1^2 \frac{1}{x-3} - \frac{1}{x+2}$ dx by algebra.

Explain why the two integrals have the same answer.

The discussion point illustrates an important technique for integrating certain polynomial fractions – splitting a single polynomial fraction into simpler fractions which can then be integrated. This process is known as splitting the fraction into **partial fractions**.

E X A M P L E 4

Express $\dfrac{3x+1}{x+2}$ in the form $A + \dfrac{B}{x+2}$ and hence solve $\displaystyle\int \frac{3x+1}{x+2}$ dx.

S O L U T I O N

$$\frac{3x+1}{x+2} = \frac{3x+6-5}{x+2} = \frac{3x+6}{x+2} - \frac{5}{x+2} = 3 - \frac{5}{x+2}$$

Hence $\displaystyle\int \frac{3x+1}{x+2}\, dx = \int 3 - \frac{5}{x+2}\, dx$

$$= 3x - 5\,\ln|x+2| + c$$

Use a similar method to find $\displaystyle\int \frac{4x-3}{2x+1}$ dx.

EXAMPLE 5

Express $\dfrac{3x-8}{(x+6)(2x-1)}$ in the form $\dfrac{A}{x+6}+\dfrac{B}{2x-1}$.

Hence find $\displaystyle\int \dfrac{3x-8}{(x+6)(2x-1)}\ dx$.

SOLUTION

$$\frac{A}{x+6}+\frac{B}{2x-1}=\frac{A(2x-1)+B(x+6)}{(x+6)(2x-1)}$$

If $\dfrac{A(2x-1)+B(x+6)}{(x+6)(2x-1)}=\dfrac{3x-8}{(x+6)(2x-1)}$

then $A(2x-1)+B(x+6)=3x-8$ ①

Putting $x=\frac{1}{2}$ in equation ① to eliminate A gives:

$\quad 6\frac{1}{2}B=-6\frac{1}{2} \Rightarrow B=-1$

Putting $x=-6$ in equation ① to eliminate B gives:

$\quad -13A=-26 \Rightarrow A=2$

Thus $\displaystyle\int \dfrac{3x-8}{(x+6)(2x-1)}\ dx = \int \dfrac{2}{x+6}-\dfrac{1}{2x-1}\ dx$

$$= 2\ln|x+6| - \tfrac{1}{2}\ln|2x-1| + c$$

EXERCISE 4

1 Split into partial fractions:

(a) $\dfrac{x}{(x+2)(x+3)}$

(b) $\dfrac{3}{(2x+1)(x+1)}$

(c) $\dfrac{x+7}{2x^2+3x-2}$

(d) $\dfrac{7x-12}{(x-1)(x-2)}$

(e) $\dfrac{5x+4}{(2x+1)(3x+2)}$

(f) $\dfrac{x-1}{x(x+1)}$

2 (a) Express $\dfrac{5x+1}{x^2-x-12}$ in the form $\dfrac{A}{x+3}+\dfrac{B}{x-4}$.

(b) Hence find $\displaystyle\int \dfrac{5x+1}{x^2-x-12}\ dx$.

3 Rewrite $\dfrac{x^2 + 8x + 9}{x^2 + 3x + 2}$ in the form $A + \dfrac{px + q}{x^2 + 3x + 2}$

and then in the form $A + \dfrac{B}{x + 1} + \dfrac{C}{x + 2}$.

Hence evaluate $\displaystyle\int_0^1 \dfrac{x^2 + 8x + 9}{x^2 + 3x + 2}\, \mathrm{d}x$.

After working through this chapter you should:

1 understand how to use the technique of integration by parts;

2 know how integration by parts and the product rule for differentiation are related;

3 understand how to use the technique of substitution for integration;

4 know that integration by substitution and the chain rule for differentiation are the same;

5 understand why it is necessary to use the absolute value of the function in the result:

$$\int \frac{f'(x)}{f(x)}\, \mathrm{d}x = \ln|f(x)| + c$$

6 know how to split a polynomial fraction into partial fractions so that the function can be integrated.

By parts

1 To find $\int e^x \cos x \, dx$ you could start as follows.

Let $u = e^x$ and $\dfrac{dv}{dx} = \cos x$

So $\int e^x \cos x \, dx = e^x \sin x - \int e^x \sin x \, dx$

If $I = \int e^x \cos x \, dx$, then:

$$I = e^x \sin x - \int e^x \sin x \, dx$$

Using integration by parts again, you should find that I appears on the right-hand side. Show how this enables you to find I.

2 Find $\int e^x \cos x \, dx$ by first putting $u = \cos x$ and $\dfrac{dv}{dx} = e^x$.

Discuss whether the choice of u and $\dfrac{dv}{dx}$ makes any difference to integrating this product.

3 Integrate each of these functions:

    (a) $e^x \sin x$ (b) $e^{2x} \cos x$ (c) $e^x \sin 2x$ (d) $e^{0.5x} \cos 2x$

4 (a) Use integration by parts to find $\int \sin x \cos x \, dx$.

    (b) You could integrate $\sin x \cos x$ by using the chain rule in reverse or by first using a trigonometric formula to rewrite $\sin x \cos x$ in a simpler form. Work out the integral by these methods and check that the answers are consistent with the one you obtained in part (a).

5 To find $\int \ln x \, dx$, write $\ln x = \ln x \times 1$ and integrate by parts, letting $u = \ln x$ and $\dfrac{dv}{dx} = 1$.

Evaluate $\int_{2}^{3} \ln x \, dx$ and draw a sketch to show the area you have worked out.

Integrating the circle

2E

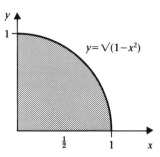

1 Explain why $\int_0^1 \sqrt{(1-x^2)}\,dx = \frac{1}{4}\pi$

It is not so easy to evaluate $\int_0^{\frac{1}{2}} \sqrt{(1-x^2)}\,dx$. This integral can, however, be integrated using the method of substitution.

2 (a) The obvious substitution to try would be $u = 1 - x^2$. What happens when you try this substitution?

(b) Try the trigonometric substitution, $\sin\theta = x$, and show that:

$$\int \sqrt{(1-x^2)}\,dx = \int \cos^2\theta\,d\theta$$
$$= \frac{1}{2}x\sqrt{(1-x^2)} + \frac{1}{2}\sin^{-1}x + c$$

(Hint: Use the identity $2\cos^2\theta = 1 + \cos 2\theta$.)

(c) Confirm that $\int_0^1 \sqrt{(1-x^2)}\,dx = \frac{1}{4}\pi$ and evaluate $\int_0^{\frac{1}{2}} \sqrt{(1-x^2)}\,dx$.

There is a more elegant way of evaluating a definite integral than using the method of substitution, and that is to substitute the limits at the same time as you substitute the function.

3 If $\sin u = x$, explain why $x = 0$ if $\theta = 0$ and why $x = \frac{1}{2}$ if $\theta = \frac{1}{6}\pi$.

Thus $\int_0^{\frac{1}{2}} \sqrt{(1-x^2)}\,dx = \int_0^{\frac{1}{6}\pi} \cos^2\theta\,d\theta$

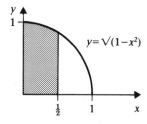

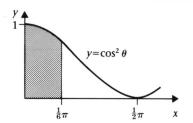

The two shaded areas are precisely equal.

4 Evaluate $\int_0^{\frac{1}{6}\pi} \cos^2 \theta \, d\theta$ and confirm your answer to 2(c).

5 (a) Give a geometrical reason
     why the triangle OAB has
     area $= \frac{1}{8}\sqrt{3}$ and why
     the sector OBC has area $= \frac{1}{12}\pi$.

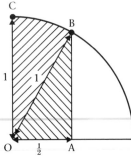

   (b) Do these results agree with the answer you found by integration?

6 Use the method of substitution to evaluate $\int_{1.5}^{3} \sqrt{(9 - x^2)} \, dx$.

7 Use the trigonometric substitution, $\tan u = x$, to evaluate $\int \dfrac{1}{1 + x^2} \, dx$.

   (Hint: Use the identity $1 + \tan^2 \theta = \sec^2 \theta$.)

8 Use the trigonometric substitution $\sin u = x$ to evaluate:

$$\int \frac{1}{\sqrt{(1 - x^2)}} \, dx$$

9 Repeat question 8 but use the substitution $\cos v = x$.

10 Use a graph plotter to graph, on the same axes, the graphs of:

   (a) $y = \sin^{-1} x$ (b) $y = -\cos^{-1} x$

   How do these graphs explain the apparent discrepancy in your answers to
   questions 8 and 9?

5 Polynomial approximations

5.1 Taylor's first approximation

You can determine the value of a function such as $\sin x$ or e^x for whatever value of x you choose, merely by pressing the appropriate button on a calculator. You may, however, have wondered how the calculator computes these values. When a computer evaluates a function such as $\sin x$, it does so by evaluating a polynomial approximation to the function. This chapter will look at how you can obtain and make use of polynomial approximations in order to solve equations and handle complicated functions.

The simplest polynomial approximation to a function is linear. You will recall that a differentiable function always appears to be locally straight under sufficient magnification and it is because of this that the first approximation of a function at a point is taken to be the tangent to the graph of the function at that point.

Such an approximation is known as **Taylor's first approximation**, after the English mathematician, Brook Taylor (1685–1731).

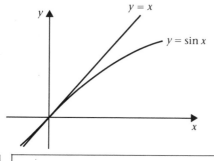

For example:

$$y = x$$

is Taylor's first approximation to

$$y = \sin x \quad \text{near the origin}$$

(a) Using radians, obtain values of x and $\sin x$ for small x. For what range of x would you consider $y = x$ to be a reasonable approximation to $y = \sin x$?

(b) Is the approximation '$\sin x \approx x$ for small values of x' valid if x is an angle measured in degrees? Explain your answer.

(c) Find a similar approximation for: (i) $\tan x$ (ii) $\cos x$

Taylor's first approximation is often used as a 'rule of thumb'. For example, you will sometimes find it useful to say that '$\sin x = x$ when x is small', although $\sin x$ is actually equal to x only when $x = 0$.

For small x, $\sin x \approx x$ $\cos x \approx 1$ $\tan x \approx x$

where x is measured in radians.

It is possible to find a Taylor approximation at a point other than the origin. The process simply involves finding the equation of the tangent at the given point.

EXAMPLE 1

Find Taylor's first approximation to the function $y = \sin x$ when $x = \frac{1}{6}\pi$.

SOLUTION

The point P on $y = \sin x$ has coordinates $(\frac{1}{6}\pi, \frac{1}{2})$, i.e. (0.52, 0.5).

Since $\dfrac{dy}{dx} = \cos x$, the gradient of the graph at P is $\cos \frac{1}{6}\pi = 0.87$.

The equation of the tangent at P is given by:

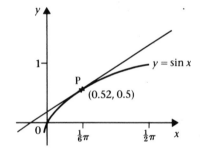

$$\frac{y - 0.5}{x - 0.52} = 0.87$$

$$\Rightarrow \quad y - 0.5 = 0.87(x - 0.52)$$
$$\Rightarrow \quad\quad\quad y = 0.87x + 0.05$$

which is Taylor's first approximation.

Plot the function on a graph plotter and superimpose Taylor's first approximation. For what range of values is the approximation a good one?

EXERCISE 1

1   Find Taylor's first approximations to the following functions at the points given. Check your answers using a graph plotter.

(a) $y = x^3 + 5x - 2$ at (2, 16)   (b) $y = e^x$ at (0, 1)   (c) $y = \ln x$ at (1, 0)

(d) $y = x^4 - x^2$ at (2, 12)   (e) $y = x^2 + \ln x$ at (1, 1)

2E   (a) Find Taylor's first approximation to $y = \cos x$ at $x = \frac{1}{2}\pi$.

(b) Use your approximation to estimate cos 1.5 to 6 decimal places.

(c) What is the percentage error in your estimate?

5.2 The Newton–Raphson method

Taking a tangent as an approximation to a function has an extremely useful application. The contemporary and colleague of Isaac Newton, Joseph Raphson (1648–1715) realised that it was possible to use a tangent approximation to a curve in order to solve virtually **any** equation quickly and rapidly using an iterative approach.

Techniques for solving equations using iterative methods are covered in *Foundations*. Whilst in some cases they can be quick and easy to use, in other cases they are slow and unreliable. The Newton–Raphson method, although using a more complex formula, is usually both fast and reliable.

All iterative methods require a first approximation to a root, which will normally be obtained by doing a quick sketch of the graph. The method can be illustrated by looking at a specific problem, such as solving $x^2 - 3 \sin x = 0$.

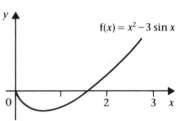

$f(x) = x^2 - 3 \sin x$

From the graph, it can be seen that $x = 2$ is a reasonable first approximation to the root. At $x = 2$, $f(2) = 4 - 3 \sin 2 = 1.27$ and, since $f'(x) = 2x - 3 \cos x$, the gradient of the tangent is $f'(2) = 4 - 3 \cos 2 = 5.25$.

Using the method of section 5.1, Taylor's first approximation is $y = 5.25x - 9.23$.

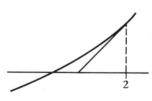

By enlarging the region around the root it can be seen that a better approximation can be found where the tangent at $x = 2$ cuts the x-axis, i.e. where $5.25x - 9.23 = 0$. This gives $x = 1.758$.

This method will generalise to give a formula for the improved approximation.

Suppose the equation to be solved is $f(x) = 0$ and the root you are trying to find is α.
If $x = a$ is the first guess and the tangent at $x = a$ crosses the x-axis at $x = b$, then $x = b$ will be closer to the actual solution α than was $x = a$.

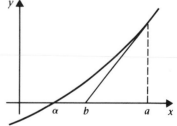

Show that $f'(a) = \dfrac{f(a)}{a - b}$ and hence that $b = a - \dfrac{f(a)}{f'(a)}$.

You can now use this 'improved guess' as the starting value in the process and hence obtain a value for x which is even closer to the root. So if you repeat the process several times you can get closer and closer to the solution of $f(x) = 0$.

TASKSHEET 1 — The Newton–Raphson method (page 75)

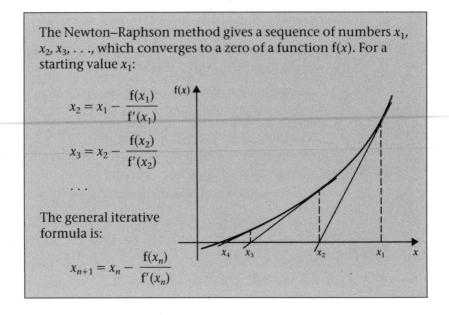

The Newton–Raphson method gives a sequence of numbers x_1, x_2, x_3, . . ., which converges to a zero of a function $f(x)$. For a starting value x_1:

$$x_2 = x_1 - \frac{f(x_1)}{f'(x_1)}$$

$$x_3 = x_2 - \frac{f(x_2)}{f'(x_2)}$$

. . .

The general iterative formula is:

$$x_{n+1} = x_n - \frac{f(x_n)}{f'(x_n)}$$

Providing the first estimate, x_1, is 'good', the method will usually converge to a zero of the function very quickly. A good first estimate is one such that the graph is locally straight at all points between the zero and the estimate, and has no turning points. If the initial estimate is itself near a turning point, the Newton–Raphson method will usually take you further from the zero, and becomes unpredictable.

In practice, not all equations are of the form:

$$f(x) = 0$$

Sometimes an equation will take the form:

$$h(x) = g(x)$$

Such an equation can always be rearranged into the form:

$$h(x) - g(x) = 0$$

and so the problem becomes one of finding the zero of the function, $h(x) - g(x)$.

EXAMPLE 2

Solve $\sin 2x = x^2$.

SOLUTION

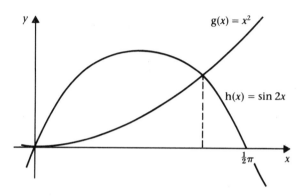

This equation cannot be solved algebraically, so a numerical method must be used.

The sketch shows that there are two solutions.

$x = 0$ is one solution, and the other is somewhere between $x = 0$ and $x = \frac{1}{2}\pi$.

This suggests a possible value of $x_1 = 1$.

The equation can be expressed in the form $f(x) = 0$ by writing:

$$x^2 - \sin 2x = 0$$

Then $f(x) = x^2 - \sin 2x$ and $f'(x) = 2x - 2\cos 2x$

Hence the iteration formula will be $x_{n+1} = x_n - \dfrac{x_n^2 - \sin 2x_n}{2x_n - 2\cos 2x_n}$.

Taking $x_1 = 1$, $x_2 = 0.967976$, $x_3 = 0.966878$, $x_4 = 0.966877$ and $x_5 = 0.966877$. Since x_4 and x_5 agree to 6 decimal places, you can conclude that $x = 0.966877$ to 6 decimal places.

The Newton–Raphson method is usually extremely efficient. You will often find that if x_1 is accurate to 1 decimal place, then x_2 is accurate to 2 decimal places, x_3 to 4 decimal places, x_4 to 8 decimal places and x_5 to 16 decimal places!

EXERCISE 2

1 Solve $x = \cos x$ correct to 6 decimal places. How can you be sure there is only one root to this equation?

2 Use the Newton–Raphson method to find the three roots of $x^3 = 3x - 1$ to 6 decimal places.

3 Find the positive solution of $e^{2x} = 3 \cos x$ correct to 6 decimal places.

4 A circular disc, centre O, is divided by a straight cut AB so that the smaller area ACB is $\frac{1}{10}$ the area of the whole circle.

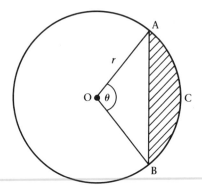

Show that, if angle AOB $= \theta$ radians, then $\theta - \frac{1}{5}\pi = \sin \theta$.

Solve the equation and find θ correct to 3 decimal places.

5E

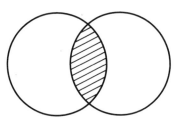

Two circles of radius r intersect as shown. The angle subtended by the common chord at the centre of each circle is 2θ.

(a) Find an expression for the shaded area in terms of r and θ.

(b) If the shaded area is equal to $\frac{1}{4}$ of the area of one of the two circles, show that $8\theta - 4 \sin 2\theta = \pi$ and hence find θ to 4 decimal places.

6E Two savers each have a regular income to invest. Tom invests in a savings account and calculates that after t years his savings will be worth £5000 ($e^{0.1t} - 1$). Jerry invests in life assurance and he estimates that after t years his savings will be worth £700t (1 + 0.06t).

(a) Who has more savings:

    (i) in the short term;

    (ii) in the long term?

(b) After how long will Tom's and Jerry's savings be equal? (Give your answer in years and months.)

5.3 Quadratic approximations

To calculate the equation of a linear function, you need to know either two points on the graph or one point and the gradient of the graph at that point.

> (a) What sort of information is needed to calculate the equation of a quadratic function?
>
> (b) How many different quadratic functions, $p(x) = a + bx + cx^2$, can you find which pass through the point $(0, 10)$ with gradient 4?

If you plot your equations on a graph plotter, they all pass through the same point $(0, 10)$ and they all have the same gradient (4) at that point. However, you will notice that some of the graphs are more **curved** than others. In fact it is the rate at which the gradient is increasing or decreasing which is different for each of them. The rate at which a gradient is increasing or decreasing is easily calculated. You simply find the gradient of the gradient graph. In other words, differentiate the function twice.

> The symbol $f''(x)$ is used when the function is differentiated twice, $f^{(3)}(x)$ is used when the function is differentiated three times, $f^{(4)}(x)$ when the function is differentiated four times, etc.
>
> For example:
> $$f(x) = a + bx + cx^2$$
> $$\Rightarrow f'(x) = b + 2cx$$
> $$\Rightarrow f''(x) = 2c$$
>
> The Leibnitz notation for $f^{(n)}(x)$ is $\dfrac{d^n y}{dx^n}$ $\left(\text{i.e., } f''(x) = \dfrac{d^2 y}{dx^2}\right)$.

> If $f(x) = \cos x$, then $f(0) = 1$, $f'(0) = 0$ and $f''(0) = -1$. Find the quadratic function $p(x) = a + bx + cx^2$ for which $p(0) = 1$, $p'(0) = 0$ and $p''(0) = -1$.

The function $p(x)$ in the thinking point above is called the quadratic approximation to $\cos x$ at $x = 0$.

> Find the quadratic approximation to $f(x) = e^x$ at $x = 0$.

5.4 Maclaurin's series

Taylor's first approximation to a function at a point is a linear function which passes through the point with the same gradient as the function. A better approximation to a function can be found by using a quadratic graph. For example, the graph of $p(x) = 1 - \frac{1}{2}x^2$ is a good approximation to $f(x) = \cos x$, whilst $p(x) = 1 + x + \frac{1}{2}x^2$ is a good approximation to $f(x) = e^x$.

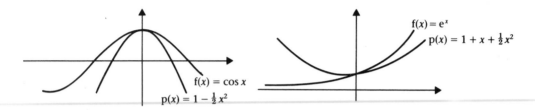

$f(x) = e^x$

$p(x) = 1 + x + \frac{1}{2}x^2$

$f(x) = \cos x$

$p(x) = 1 - \frac{1}{2}x^2$

Comparing the properties of the function $f(x) = \cos x$ with its approximating quadratic $p(x) = 1 - \frac{1}{2}x^2$ gives:

- $f(0) = 1, \qquad p(0) = 1$
  i.e. they are equal at $x = 0$.

- $f'(x) = -\sin x \Rightarrow f'(0) = 0, \qquad p'(x) = -x \Rightarrow p'(0) = 0$
  i.e. their gradients are equal to $x = 0$.

- $f''(x) = -\cos x \Rightarrow f''(0) = -1, \qquad p''(x) = -1 \Rightarrow p''(0) = -1$
  i.e. their second derivatives are equal at $x = 0$.

(a) Compare the function e^x and its derivatives at $x = 0$ with $1 + x + \frac{1}{2}x^2$ and its derivatives at $x = 0$.

(b) Even better approximations can be obtained with cubics. What do you think are the properties of a cubic approximation?

(c) What would be the properties of a fourth degree, a fifth degree and an nth degree approximation?

TASKSHEET 2 — Finding the polynomial (page 77)

If a function $f(x)$ can be differentiated n times at $x = 0$, then a polynomial of degree n which has the same derivatives as the function will be a good approximation to the function for values of x near zero.

The result developed in tasksheet 2 was published by Colin Maclaurin (1698–1746). Maclaurin was a Professor of Mathematics at Aberdeen by the age of nineteen and a Fellow of the Royal Society at twenty-one. In 1742 he published his book *Treatise on Fluxions*, which included a description of the 'Maclaurin series'. He took part in opposing the march of the Young Pretender when the Jacobites attacked Edinburgh in 1745 and when the city fell he fled to York, where he died. Despite its name, Maclaurin's series was first used by James Stirling.

Maclaurin's series

If $f(x)$ can be differentiated n times at $x = 0$, then the approximation:

$$f(x) = f(0) + f'(0)x + \frac{f''(0)x^2}{2!} + \frac{f^{(3)}(0)x^3}{3!} + \frac{f^{(4)}(0)x^4}{4!} + \ldots$$
$$+ \frac{f^{(n)}(0)x^n}{n!}$$

will be good for values of x close to $x = 0$.

If you write the series out so that all terms are of the form $\dfrac{f^{(r)}(0)x^r}{r!}$, the

first three terms become: $\dfrac{f(0)x^0}{0!} + \dfrac{f'(0)x^1}{1!} + \dfrac{f''(0)x^2}{2!} + \ldots$

What value does this suggest 0! should have? Check your suggestion using a calculator.

EXAMPLE 4

(a) Find the Maclaurin's series for $\sin x$.

(b) Use the series found in (a) to find the series for $\sin (x^2)$.

SOLUTION

(a) If $\begin{aligned} f(x) &= \sin x & \text{then} && f(0) &= 0 \\ f'(x) &= \cos x & \Rightarrow && f'(0) &= 1 \\ f''(x) &= -\sin x & \Rightarrow && f''(0) &= 0 \\ f^{(3)}(x) &= -\cos x & \Rightarrow && f^{(3)}(0) &= -1 \\ f^{(4)}(x) &= \sin x & \Rightarrow && f^{(4)}(0) &= 0 \\ f^{(5)}(x) &= \cos x & \Rightarrow && f^{(5)}(0) &= 1 \end{aligned}$ and the cycle repeats itself.

71

Thus, using the values for f(0), f'(0), f''(0), . . ., Maclaurin's series will be:

$$f(0) + f'(0)x + \frac{f''(0)x^2}{2!} + \frac{f^{(3)}(0)x^3}{3!} + \frac{f^{(4)}(0)x^4}{4!} + \ldots + \frac{f^{(7)}(0)x^7}{7!} +$$

$$= 0 + 1x + \frac{0x^2}{2!} - \frac{1x^3}{3!} + \frac{0x^4}{4!} + \frac{1x^5}{5!} + \frac{0x^6}{6!} - \frac{1x^7}{7!} + \ldots$$

$$\Rightarrow \sin x = x - \frac{x^3}{3!} + \frac{x^5}{5!} - \frac{x^7}{7!} + \frac{x^9}{9!} - \ldots$$

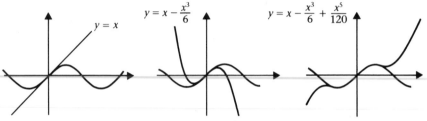

(b) You can use the series $\sin x = x - \dfrac{x^3}{3!} + \dfrac{x^5}{5!} - \dfrac{x^7}{7!} + \ldots$

to find the series for $\sin x^2$ by replacing x by x^2.

Thus $\sin (x^2) = x^2 - \dfrac{(x^2)^3}{3!} + \dfrac{(x^2)^5}{5!} - \dfrac{(x^2)^7}{7!} + \ldots$

$$= x^2 - \frac{x^6}{3!} + \frac{x^{10}}{5!} - \frac{x^{14}}{7!}$$

(a) Use a graph plotter to superimpose the graphs of:

$$y = \sin x \quad \text{and} \quad y = x - \frac{x^3}{3!} + \frac{x^5}{5!} - \frac{x^7}{7!} + \frac{x^9}{9!}$$

How good an approximation is the polynomial to the sine wave?

(b) Explain why $\cos x = 1 - \dfrac{x^2}{2!} + \dfrac{x^4}{4!} - \dfrac{x^6}{6!} + \ldots$

(c) Find the series for e^x.

These results are important and worth recording. The binomial series which you have already met can be obtained using Maclaurin's series. Another important series is that for ln $(1 + x)$, which is developed in tasksheet 3E.

TASKSHEET 3E — Some proofs (page 78)

Not all series are valid for all values of x. For example, although:

$$\frac{1}{1+x} = 1 - x + x^2 - x^3 + x^4 \ldots \text{ for values of } x \text{ between } -1 \text{ and } 1$$

when x is put equal to 2 the result:

$$\frac{1}{1+2} = 1 - 2 + 4 - 8 + 16 \ldots$$

is clearly untrue!

$$\sin x = x - \frac{x^3}{3!} + \frac{x^5}{5!} - \frac{x^7}{7!} + \ldots \qquad \text{(all } x)$$

$$\cos x = 1 - \frac{x^2}{2!} + \frac{x^4}{4!} - \frac{x^6}{6!} + \ldots \qquad \text{(all } x)$$

$$e^x = 1 + x + \frac{x^2}{2!} + \frac{x^3}{3!} + \frac{x^4}{4!} + \ldots \qquad \text{(all } x)$$

$$\ln(1 + x) = x - \frac{x^2}{2} + \frac{x^3}{3} - \frac{x^4}{4} + \ldots \qquad (-1 < x \leqslant 1)$$

$$(1 + x)^n = 1 + nx + \frac{n(n-1)}{2!}x^2 + \frac{n(n-1)(n-2)}{3!}x^3 + \ldots$$

$$(-1 < x < 1)$$

EXERCISE 3

1 Find the first five terms of the Maclaurin's series for e^{2x}:

(a) by differentiation and evaluation of f(0), f'(0), . . .;

(b) by substituting into the series $e^x = 1 + x + \frac{x^2}{2!} + \frac{x^3}{3!} + \ldots$

2 Use the expansion of e^x to evalue e^1 to 12 decimal places.

3 (a) Use your calculator to find cos 0.5.

(b) How many terms of the cosine series are needed to give an answer that is accurate to ±0.001?

(c) How many terms of the cosine series are needed to give cos 1.0 to an accuracy of ±0.001?

4 Write down the nth term of the series for each of the functions:

(a) e^x (b) $\cos x$ (c) e^{x^2}

5 (a) Find the Maclaurin's series for $\ln(1 - x)$.

(b) Use the result $1 - x^2 = (1 - x)(1 + x)$, together with a property of logs, to find the series for $\ln(1 - x^2)$.

6 (a) Show that $e^{-x} \approx 1 - x$.

(b) Use your result in (a) to show that $\sqrt{(1 - e^{-x})} \approx \sqrt{x}$.

(c) What is the percentage error in using $\sqrt{x}$ as an approximation to $\sqrt{(1 - e^{-x})}$ when $x = 0.1$?

After working through this chapter you should:

1 be able to find Taylor's first approximation to a function;

2 know the Newton–Raphson method for solving equations;

3 be able to find second and higher derivatives and be familiar with the notation:

$$f'(x), f''(x), f^{(3)}(x), f^{(4)}(x), \ldots, f^{(n)}(x)$$

4 be able to use a Maclaurin's series to find a polynomial approximation to a function;

5 know the Maclaurin's series of particular functions such as $\sin x$, $\cos x$, e^x, $\ln(1 + x)$ and $(1 + x)^n$ and know the range of x for which these series are valid.

The Newton–Raphson method

You have seen that, if $x = a$ is an approximation to the solution of $f(x) = 0$, then $b = a - \dfrac{f(a)}{f'(a)}$ appears to be a better approximation.

1   For the equation $x^2 - 3 \sin x = 0$ you know there is a solution near $x = 2$.

(a) If $f(x) = x^2 - 3 \sin x$, write down $f'(x)$.

(b) Use the formula, $b = a - \dfrac{f(a)}{f'(a)}$ with $a = 2$, to obtain a better approximation to the root.

(c) Taking your improved approximation in (b) as your new value for (a), find a new approximation.

(d) Continue this process until you have an estimate of the root which is accurate to 6 decimal places.

2

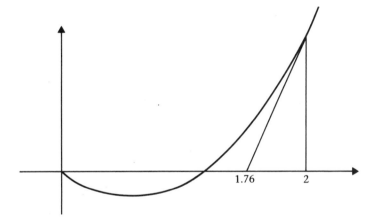

The diagram shows how the second approximation, 1.76, is obtained geometrically from the first approximation, $a = 2$. Copy the diagram and show how the third and fourth approximations can be constructed.

The Newton–Raphson process generates an iterative sequence, $x_1, x_2, x_3, x_4, \ldots, x_n$, and the equation:

$$b = a - \frac{f(a)}{f'(a)}$$

can be written as:

$$x_{n+1} = x_n - \frac{f(x_n)}{f'(x_n)}$$

75

3 (a) Sketch the graph of $f(x) = x^2 - 6 + 6e^{-x}$.

   (b) Find a suitable first approximation x_1 to the positive root of the equation:

   $$x^2 - 6 + 6e^{-x} = 0$$

   (c) Write down $f'(x)$ and hence give the Newton–Raphson formula.

   (d) Use the Newton–Raphson formula to find the root correct to 4 decimal places.

Although the Newton–Raphson process is generally efficient, it can give rise to problems. The next example illustrates one such problem.

4

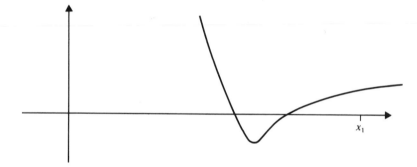

Copy the diagram and use the method of question 2 to show how to construct the approximations x_2, x_3 from the starting value of x_1 given. Why is Newton–Raphson not appropriate in this case?

5E (a) Use a computer or calculator with function $f(x) = 30 - 15x - 2x^2 + x^3$ and $x_1 = 5$ to solve the equation $30 - 15x - 2x^2 + x^3 = 0$.

   Help is given on technology datasheet: *Newton–Raphson*.

   (b) Do other starting values work? Can you find any that do not? What happens if $x_1 = 3$, 3.1, 2.8, 2.9?

   (c) What range of start values converges to the root $x = 2$?

   (d) What happens when (i) $x_1 = -0.68$, (ii) $x_1 = -0.69$?

   (e) Change the function and solve $5 \cos x - x = 0$ with starting values
   (i) $x_1 = -1$, (ii) $x_1 = -0.5$, (iii) $x_1 = -7$, (iv) $x_1 = -6.5$.
   Comment on your results.

   (f) Change the function to $2\sqrt{x} - 1 = 0$. Can you find a suitable starting point?

6E Try to solve $\sin x - \frac{1}{50} \sin(100x) = 0$, with starting values $x = 1$, 2 or 3. Zoom in on the curve and explain what is happening.

Finding the polynomial

You have seen that when you approximate to a function $f(x)$ using the quadratic $p(x) = a + bx + cx^2$, you have to solve:

$$f(0) = a \qquad f'(0) = b \qquad f''(0) = 2c$$

To extend this method to general polynomials, you have to solve more equations of this form.

1 If $p(x) = a + bx + cx^2 + dx^3$ and $p(0) = 12$, $p'(0) = 11$, $p''(0) = 10$ and $p^{(3)}(0) = 6$, find a, b, c and d.

2 If $p(x) = a + bx + cx^2 + dx^3$ express a, b, c and d in terms of $p(0)$, $p'(0)$, $p''(0)$ and $p^{(3)}(0)$ and hence show that $p(x) = p(0) + p'(0)x + p''(0)\,\dfrac{x^2}{2} + p^{(3)}(0)\,\dfrac{x^3}{6}$.

3 Explain why, if $p(x)$ is a polynomial of degree four, then:

$$p(x) = p(0) + p'(0)x + p''(0)\,\frac{x^2}{2!} + p^{(3)}(0)\,\frac{x^3}{3!} + p^{(4)}(0)\,\frac{x^4}{4!}$$

4 (a) In a similar way, if $p(x)$ is a polynomial of degree five write down $p(x)$ in terms of its derivatives at $x = 0$.

   (b) Generalise this result to a polynomial of degree n.

5 If $f(x) = e^{2x}$, find $f(0)$, $\quad f'(0)$, $\quad f''(0)$, $\quad f^{(3)}(0)$, $\quad f^{(4)}(0)$.

Hence explain why $1 + 2x + \dfrac{2^2 x^2}{2!} + \dfrac{2^3 x^3}{3!} + \dfrac{2^4 x^4}{4!}$ is a good approximation to e^{2x} for values of x near $x = 0$.

Plot both of these functions on a graph plotter and suggest a range of x-values for which the approximation is good.

Some proofs

For this tasksheet you will need to use the results:

$$\frac{d}{dx}(\ln(1+x)) = \frac{1}{1+x}$$

$$\frac{d}{dx}((1+x)^n) = n(1+x)^{n-1}$$

For example:

$$\frac{d}{dx}\left(\frac{1}{(1+x)^2}\right) = \frac{d}{dx}((1+x)^{-2}) = -2(1+x)^{-3}$$

1   (a) If $f(x) = \ln x$, explain what happens if you attempt to evaluate $f(0)$.

(b) Explain why it is not possible to find a Maclaurin's series for $\ln x$.

For the reason given in question 1, $\ln x$ does not have a series expansion. The series for $\ln(1+x)$ is found instead.

2   (a) If $f(x) = \ln(1+x)$, write down $f'(x)$.

(b) By writing $\dfrac{1}{1+x}$ as $(1+x)^{-1}$, write down $f''(x)$.

(c) Show that $f^{(3)}(x) = 2(1+x)^{-3}$ and find $f^{(4)}(x)$ and $f^{(5)}(x)$.

(d) Find $f(0)$, $f'(0)$, $f''(0)$, $f^{(3)}(0)$, $f^{(4)}(0)$ and $f^{(5)}(0)$.

(e) Show that the Maclaurin's series for $\ln(1+x)$ is:

$$x - \frac{x^2}{2} + \frac{x^3}{3} - \frac{x^4}{4} + \frac{x^5}{5}\ldots$$

3   (a) If $f(x) = (1+x)^n$, write down $f'(x)$.

(b) Write down $f''(x)$ and show that $f^{(3)}(x) = n(n-1)(n-2)(1+x)^{n-3}$.

(c) Use the results from parts (a) and (b) to show that the first four terms of $(1+x)^n$ are:

$$1 + nx + \frac{n(n-1)}{2!}x^2 + \frac{n(n-1)(n-2)}{3!}x^3$$

6 First principles

6.1 Zooming in

Your study of calculus has been based upon the idea of local straightness. When you zoom in at a point on a locally straight curve, the curve appears to be a straight line and this enables you to find the gradient.

However, zooming in does not always make a curve appear straight. From a spaceship, the Earth appears to have a smooth, spherical surface, but from a closer vantage point, enormous imperfections in the surface are apparent.

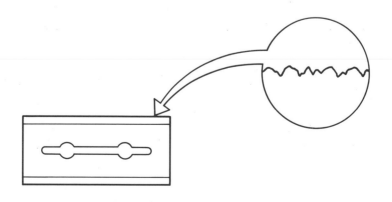

Use a graph plotter to plot the graph of:

$$y = x + \tfrac{1}{1000} \sin (1000x)$$

Investigate what happens as you zoom in on any point of the graph.

To be able to differentiate a function you require the graph of the function to be locally straight, but so far you have no way of knowing whether a graph really is locally straight. For example, in the thinking point above, the appearance of the graph changed dramatically as you zoomed in at a chosen point. So you cannot be totally sure whether or not the appearance would change again if you zoomed in further.

One important mathematical activity concerns giving rigorous arguments to prove results indisputibly. It seems that you would have to zoom in forever in order to confirm that graphs of relations such as $y = \sin x$ or $y = x^2$ really **are** locally straight. The mathematical technique for doing this is studied in the discussion point and the next section.

To be able to find the numerical gradient of $y = x^2$ at the point (3, 9) you have previously considered the gradients of lines joining (3, 9) to nearby points on the graph.

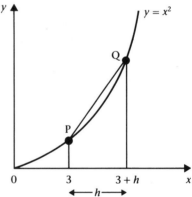

P is the point $(3, 3^2)$ and Q has x-coordinate $3 + h$.

(a) What is the y-coordinate of Q?

(b) What is the difference between the y-coordinates of Q and P?

(c) Find the gradient of PQ. (Simplify the expression as far as possible.)

(d) As h becomes smaller and smaller, what happens to the value of the gradient?

(e) What is the advantage of using the letter h rather than a small numerical value?

6.2 Limits

In the opening section of this chapter you considered the value $6 + h$ as h becomes smaller. Making the value of h smaller and smaller is termed 'letting h tend to zero' and the notation for this is:

$$h \to 0$$

Finding the value of $6 + h$ as h tends to zero is termed 'finding the limit of $6 + h$ as h tends to zero' and the notation for this is:

$$\lim_{h \to 0} (6 + h)$$

> The limit of $6 + h$ as h tends to zero is:
>
> $$\lim_{h \to 0} (6 + h) = 6$$

TASKSHEET 1 — Limits (page 85)

On the tasksheet, you found a number of limits of the following type:

$$\lim_{h \to 0} 2(h + 3) = 6$$

A limit of the form:

$$\lim_{h \to 0} \frac{3 + h}{2 + h} = \frac{3}{2}$$

can be found simply by substituting zero for h in both numerator and denominator. However, this method cannot be applied if the denominator is zero when h is zero.

E X A M P L E   1

Find $\lim\limits_{h \to 0} \dfrac{4h - h^3}{9h + h^2}$

S O L U T I O N

For $h \neq 0$, $\quad \dfrac{4h - h^3}{9h + h^2} = \dfrac{(4 - h^2)h}{(9 + h)h} = \dfrac{4 - h^2}{9 + h}$

$\Rightarrow \lim\limits_{h \to 0} \dfrac{4h - h^3}{9h + h^2} = \dfrac{4}{9}$

6.3 Differentiating from first principles

The notation you have developed for limits can be used to give a general definition for the gradient of the graph of a function.

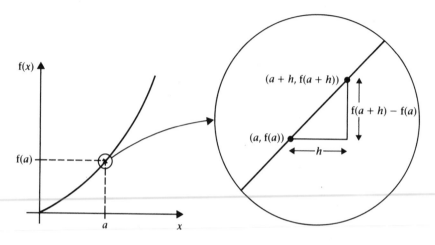

The gradient of the graph of the function f at the point $(a, f(a))$ is given by:

$$f'(a) = \lim_{h \to 0} \frac{f(a + h) - f(a)}{h}$$

(If the limit does not exist, then the function is **not** locally straight and does not have a gradient at $x = a$.)

Finding a gradient by means of the limit is called **differentiating from first principles**.

EXAMPLE 2

Differentiate $y = 3x^2 - 4x$ at $(3, 15)$ from first principles.

SOLUTION

$f(3 + h) = 3(3 + h)^2 - 4(3 + h)$
$\qquad\quad\; = 3(9 + 6h + h^2) - 12 - 4h$
$\qquad\quad\; = 15 + 14h + 3h^2$

The gradient is $\lim\limits_{h \to 0} \dfrac{\cancel{15} + 14h + 3h^2 - \cancel{15}}{h}$

$\qquad\qquad\quad = \lim\limits_{h \to 0} (14 + 3h) = 14$

For any function f, a general formula for $f'(x)$ can be found from first principles using the definition:

$$f'(x) = \lim_{h \to 0} \frac{f(x + h) - f(x)}{h}$$

E X A M P L E   3

If $y = x^2$, find $\dfrac{dy}{dx}$ from first principles.

S O L U T I O N

$$\frac{dy}{dx} = \lim_{h \to 0} \frac{(x + h)^2 - x^2}{h}$$

$$= \lim_{h \to 0} \frac{\cancel{x^2} + 2xh + h^2 - \cancel{x^2}}{h}$$

$$= \lim_{h \to 0} (2x + h) = 2x$$

E X E R C I S E   1

1   Suppose $y = 3x^2$.

(a) Find the gradient at (1, 3) from first principles.

(b) Find a general formula for $\dfrac{dy}{dx}$ from first principles.

2   Differentiate $5x^2 + 3x$ with respect to x, from first principles.

3   Differentiate $4x^2 - 2x + 7$ with respect to x, from first principles.

4E   Use first principles to find the derivative with respect to x of $\sin x$. [You can assume the limits obtained numerically on tasksheet 1.]

The method of differentiating from first principles is important, since it is the way in which mathematicians have proved all the known derivatives. It can also be used to **prove** the correctness of the various rules of differentiation.

After working through this chapter you should:

1   appreciate that you need the algebraic limit process to determine whether the graph of a function really is locally straight;

2   understand the notation $\lim_{h \to 0} f(h)$;

3   be able to evaluate simple limits;

4   know how to obtain derivatives from first principles using the expression $\lim_{h \to 0} \dfrac{f(x + h) - f(x)}{h}$

Limits

1 Evaluate: (a) $\lim_{h \to 0}(5h - 2)$ (b) $\lim_{h \to 0}(3 + 2h)$

Limits can be obtained for h tending to values other than 0.

The limit of $\dfrac{h(h - 2)}{h - 2}$ as h tends to 2 is written as $\lim_{h \to 2} \dfrac{h(h - 2)}{h - 2}$.

This limit **cannot** be evaluated simply by putting h equal to 2, because $\frac{0}{0}$ is undefined. However, for $h \neq 2$, the factor $h - 2$ can be cancelled.

$$\lim_{h \to 2} \frac{h(h - 2)}{h - 2} = \lim_{h \to 2} h$$
$$= 2$$

2 Use this method to evaluate:

(a) $\lim_{h \to 0} \dfrac{h(h + 2)}{h}$ (b) $\lim_{h \to 0} \dfrac{5h^2 - 2h}{h}$ (c) $\lim_{h \to 0} \dfrac{4h^2 - h^3}{h}$

(d) $\lim_{h \to 2} \dfrac{(h - 2)(h + 2)}{h - 2}$ (e) $\lim_{h \to -3} \dfrac{2h^2 - 18}{h + 3}$

3 Use a calculator or computer to investigate numerically the limits:

(a) $\lim_{h \to 0} \dfrac{\sin h}{h}$ (b) $\lim_{h \to 0} \dfrac{\cos h - 1}{h}$ (c) $\lim_{h \to 0} \dfrac{e^h - 1}{h}$

Solutions

1 Parameters

1.1 Curves which vary with time

1 (a)

t	0	1	2	3	4	5
x	0	20	40	60	80	100
y	90	85	70	45	10	−35

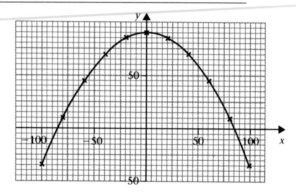

(b) Since $x = 20t$, negative values of t will simply give negative values of x and since $y = 90 - 5t^2$, the values of y will be unchanged. The result will be a graph that is symmetric about the y-axis.

(c) The curve is a parabola.

2 (a)

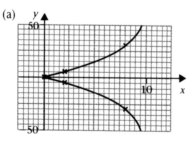

Note the symmetry in the x-axis.
Note also that, since
$x = 2t^2$, x will never be negative.

(b)

It is necessary to consider fractional values of t, for example $\frac{1}{2}, \frac{1}{3}, \frac{1}{4}$ in order to generate the arms of the hyperbola. Negative values of t result in a reflection in the origin.

1.2 Circles and ellipses

> (a) Describe what happens to x as θ varies.
>
> (b) Describe what happens to y as θ varies.
>
> (c) Explain why $(3\cos\theta)^2 + (3\sin\theta)^2 = 9$ for any value of θ and show how this connects the parametric and Cartesian equations of the circle.

(a) x oscillates between -3 and $+3$.

(b) y oscillates between -3 and $+3$.

(c) $(3\cos\theta)^2 + (3\sin\theta)^2 = 9\cos^2\theta + 9\sin^2\theta$
$$= 9$$
So, in Cartesian form, the circle has equation $x^2 + y^2 = 9$.

EXERCISE 2

1

Ellipse	Cartesian equation	Parametric equations	Area
A	$\dfrac{x^2}{9} + \dfrac{y^2}{16} = 1$	$x = 3\cos\theta$ $y = 4\sin\theta$	12π
B	$\dfrac{x^2}{9} + \dfrac{y^2}{25} = 1$	$x = 3\cos\theta$ $y = 5\sin\theta$	15π
C	$\dfrac{x^2}{0.25} + \dfrac{y^2}{0.16} = 1$	$x = 0.5\cos\theta$ $y = 0.4\sin\theta$	0.2π

2 Dividing by 36, $\dfrac{x^2}{4} + \dfrac{y^2}{9} = 1$

$x = 2\cos\theta, \quad y = 3\sin\theta$
Area $= 6\pi$

3 Dividing by 100, $\dfrac{x^2}{25} + \dfrac{y^2}{4} = 1$

$x = 5\cos\theta, \quad y = 2\sin\theta$
Area $= 10\pi$

1.3 Conversion

> Use the identity to convert the parametric equations $x = 5 \cos \theta$ and $y = 5 \sin \theta$ into the Cartesian equation $x^2 + y^2 = 25$.

$$x^2 + y^2 = 25 \cos^2\theta + 25 \sin^2 \theta$$
$$= 25 (\cos^2 \theta + \sin^2 \theta)$$
$$= 25$$

EXERCISE 3

1 $x + y = 3$

2 (a) $5x + 3y = 22$ (b) $y = 5 - \dfrac{18}{x}$ (c) $y = \dfrac{5x}{2} - \dfrac{5x^2}{16}$

3 (a) $4x^2 = 1 + \dfrac{y^2}{9}$ (b) $\dfrac{x^2}{16} + \dfrac{y^2}{9} = 1$

     (c) $(2y)^2 + 1 = x^2$ (d) $1 + (y - 1)^2 = \left(\dfrac{x}{3}\right)^3$

        $4y^2 + 1 = x^2$ $y^2 - 2y + 2 = \dfrac{x^2}{9}$

4E (a) $y = 3 + x$

     (b) Since $\sqrt{t} \geqslant 0$, it follows that $x \geqslant 1, y \geqslant 4$. Thus the parametric equations define a half-line.

5E $x = t + 2, \quad y = t^2 + 4; \quad\quad x = 2 \pm \sqrt{t}, \quad y = t + 4.$

     Many others are possible.

1.4 Differentiating parametric equations

> Use the chain rule to find $\dfrac{dy}{dx}$ when $y = \sin \theta$ and $\theta = 3x^2 + 2$.

$$\dfrac{dy}{dx} = \dfrac{dy}{d\theta} \times \dfrac{d\theta}{dx}$$
$$= \cos \theta \times 6x$$
$$= 6x \cos \theta$$
$$= 6x \cos (3x^2 + 2)$$

EXERCISE 4

1 $\dfrac{dy}{dx} = \dfrac{dy}{dt} \div \dfrac{dx}{dt}$

$\qquad = -\dfrac{1}{t^2} \div 1$

$\qquad = -\dfrac{1}{4}$ at $t = 2$

2 $\dfrac{dy}{dx} = \dfrac{4 \cos \theta}{-3 \sin \theta}$

At $\theta = \dfrac{\pi}{2}$,

$\qquad x = 0, \quad y = 4, \quad \dfrac{dy}{dx} = 0$

3 $\dfrac{dy}{dx} = \dfrac{dy}{du} \div \dfrac{dx}{du}$

$\qquad = 2u \div 4$

$\qquad = \dfrac{u}{2}$

At $u = 2$,

$\qquad x = 8, \quad y = 4, \quad \dfrac{dy}{dx} = 1$

The tangent has equation $\dfrac{y - 4}{x - 8} = 1$

$\qquad\qquad\qquad \Rightarrow y = x - 4$

4 $\dfrac{dy}{dx} = \dfrac{6u^2}{2u} = 3u$

At $u = 1$,

$\qquad x = 1, \quad y = 2, \quad \dfrac{dy}{dx} = 3$

The tangent has equation $y = 3x - 1$.

5 (a) $\dfrac{dy}{dx} = \dfrac{dy}{dv} \div \dfrac{dx}{dv}$

$\qquad = \dfrac{3v^2 - 3}{2}$

(b) $\dfrac{dy}{dx} = 0 \iff v^2 = 1$

$\qquad\qquad \iff v = \pm 1$

(c) $(2, -2)$ and $(-2, 2)$

1.5   Parametric differentiation or conversion?

1 $\dfrac{dy}{ds} = 2s$; $\dfrac{dx}{ds} = 3$, so $\dfrac{dy}{dx} = \dfrac{2s}{3}$

At $s = 1$ the gradient is $\frac{2}{3}$.

$$s = \frac{x}{3}, \quad \text{so } y = \left(\frac{x}{3}\right)^2 \quad \text{or} \quad \frac{x^2}{9}$$

$$\frac{dy}{dx} = \frac{2x}{9}$$

When $s = 1$, $x = 3$, so the gradient at $x = 3$ is $\frac{6}{9}$ or $\frac{2}{3}$.

2   (a)   Parametric differentiation is the only sensible method.

$$\frac{dy}{dt} = 3t^2; \quad \frac{dx}{dt} = 2(t+2), \quad \text{so} \quad \frac{dy}{dx} = \frac{3t^2}{2(t+2)}$$

(b)   It is easy to spot that $y = 3x - 4$,   so $\dfrac{dy}{dx} = 3$.

(c)   Parametric differentiation is the only sensible method.

$$\frac{dy}{d\theta} = 3\cos\theta; \quad \frac{dx}{d\theta} = -2\sin\theta - \cos\theta$$

$$\text{So } \frac{dy}{dx} = \frac{-3\cos\theta}{(2\sin\theta + \cos\theta)}$$

(d)   Parametric differentiation is the only method.

$$\frac{dy}{d\theta} = 3\cos 3\theta; \quad \frac{dx}{d\theta} = 2\cos 2\theta$$

$$\text{So } \frac{dy}{dx} = \frac{3\cos 3\theta}{2\cos 2\theta}$$

3E $\dfrac{dy}{dx} = \dfrac{dy}{d\theta} \div \dfrac{dx}{d\theta} = \dfrac{\cos\theta}{1 + \sin\theta}$

At $\theta = \frac{1}{4}\pi$, $(x, y) \approx (0.0783, 0.707)$ and $\dfrac{dy}{dx} \approx 0.414$

$y - 0.707 \approx 0.414\,(x - 0.0783)$
$$y \approx 0.414x + 0.675$$

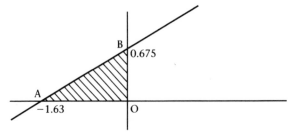

The area of the triangle is 0.550 square units.

4E $\dfrac{dy}{dx} = \dfrac{dy}{dt} \div \dfrac{dx}{dt}$

$\qquad = \dfrac{6t^2 + 4}{2t}$

$\qquad = 3t + \dfrac{2}{t}$

$\Rightarrow \left(\dfrac{dy}{dx}\right)^2 = 9t^2 + 12 + \dfrac{4}{t^2}$

Since $t^2 \geqslant 0$ for all t, $\left(\dfrac{dy}{dx}\right)^2 \geqslant 12.$

1.6   Velocity vectors

EXERCISE 6

1

t	0	1	2	3
x	0	1	4	9
y	0	3	6	9
$\mathbf{v}$	$\begin{bmatrix}0\\3\end{bmatrix}$	$\begin{bmatrix}2\\3\end{bmatrix}$	$\begin{bmatrix}4\\3\end{bmatrix}$	$\begin{bmatrix}6\\3\end{bmatrix}$
v	3	$\sqrt{13}$	5	$\sqrt{45}$

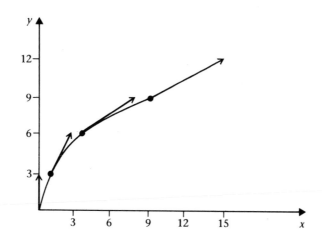

2   (a) $\mathbf{v} = \begin{bmatrix} 2t \\ 3 - 2t \end{bmatrix}$

(b) $\mathbf{v}_{t=0} = \begin{bmatrix} 0 \\ 3 \end{bmatrix}$. The speed is $3\,\mathrm{cm\,s^{-1}}$, parallel to the y-axis.

(c) $\begin{bmatrix} 2t \\ 3 - 2t \end{bmatrix} = \lambda \begin{bmatrix} 1 \\ 1 \end{bmatrix} \Rightarrow 2t = 3 - 2t$

$$\Rightarrow t = \frac{3}{4}$$

(d) $\begin{bmatrix} 2t \\ 3 - 2t \end{bmatrix} = \lambda \begin{bmatrix} 1 \\ 0 \end{bmatrix} \Rightarrow t = \frac{3}{2}$

3

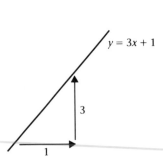

$y = 3x + 1$

The line has gradient 3. It is parallel to the vector $\begin{bmatrix} 1 \\ 3 \end{bmatrix}$, which has magnitude $\sqrt{10}$, so:

$$\mathbf{v} = \begin{bmatrix} 1 \\ 3 \end{bmatrix} \quad \text{or} \quad \begin{bmatrix} -1 \\ -3 \end{bmatrix}$$

$$\mathbf{r} = \begin{bmatrix} 0 \\ 1 \end{bmatrix} + t \begin{bmatrix} 1 \\ 3 \end{bmatrix}$$

2 Product rule

2.1 Combined functions

> Check the formula $\dfrac{dy}{dx} = u\dfrac{dv}{dx} + v\dfrac{du}{dx}$ when $u = 1 - x$ and $v = \frac{1}{2}x - 2$.

$$u\frac{dv}{dx} + v\frac{du}{dx} = \tfrac{1}{2}(1 - x) - (\tfrac{1}{2}x - 2)$$

$$= -x + 2\tfrac{1}{2}$$
$$y = (1 - x)(\tfrac{1}{2}x - 2)$$
$$= -\tfrac{1}{2}x^2 + 2\tfrac{1}{2}x - 2$$
$$\frac{dy}{dx} = -x + 2\tfrac{1}{2}$$

2.2 The product rule

EXERCISE 1

1 (a) $e^x(\sin x + \cos x)$ (b) $xe^x(2 + x)$ (c) $x^2(3\cos x - x\sin x)$

2 (a) 148   (b) 16.3

3   The gradient is sin 1.5 + 1.5 cos 1.5 = 1.1.
The equation of the tangent is $y = 1.1x - 0.16$.

4   (a) (i) $A = wh$
$$\frac{dA}{dt} = \frac{dw}{dt} \times h + w \times \frac{dh}{dt}$$
$$= 2t \sin t + t^2 \cos t$$

At $t = 1$, the rate of change of area is 2.22.

(ii) When $t = 2.5, \dfrac{dA}{dt} = -2.01$, so the area is decreasing.

(b) (i) $A = \sin t \cos t$
$$\frac{dA}{dt} = \cos^2 t - \sin^2 t$$
When $t = 0.5$ the rate of increase of area is 0.540.

(ii) The area stops increasing when $\dfrac{dA}{dt} = 0$.

So $\cos^2 t = \sin^2 t$
$\tan^2 t = 1$
This first occurs when $\tan t = 1$.
$t = \frac{1}{4}\pi = 0.785$

5   The gradient at $x = 1$ is 1.36.
The equation of the tangent is $y = 1.36x - 0.68$.

6   At the turning point, $e^x(1 + x) = 0$, so $x = -1$.
So the coordinates of the turning point are $(-1, -0.37)$.

7E   (a) At the stationary point, $e^x(2x + x^2) = 0$, so $x = 0$ or -2.
When $x = 0, y = 0$, so $(0, 0)$ is a stationary point.

(b) e^x cannot equal 0, so the only stationary points are at $x = 0$ and $x = -2$.
The coordinates of the other stationary point are $(-2, 0.54)$.

8E   (a) $0 = \dfrac{1}{x} + x\dfrac{dv}{dx}$

So $\dfrac{1}{x} = -x\dfrac{dv}{dx}$

Or $\dfrac{dv}{dx} = -\dfrac{1}{x^2}$

(b) $\dfrac{d}{dx}(x^{-1}) = (-1)x^{-2} = -\dfrac{1}{x^2}$

9E $\dfrac{dy}{dx} = \sin x + x \cos x$, so at the stationary point, $\sin x + x \cos x = 0$.
Dividing by cos x gives $\tan x + x = 0$.
One stationary point is $(0, 0)$.
The others are $(-2.03, 1.82)$ and $(2.03, 1.82)$ to 3 s.f.

2.3 Product rule and chain rule

EXERCISE 2

1 (a) $e^{3x}(6 \sin 2x + 4 \cos 2x)$

(b) $e^{2x}(2 \cos 3x - 3 \sin 3x)$

(c) $e^{x^2}(2x \sin 4x + 4 \cos 4x)$

2 (a) Chain (b) product (c) both (d) both

(e) chain (f) product (g) chain (h) both

3 (a) $\dfrac{2x}{(x^2 + 1)}$ (b) $\ln x + 1$ (c) $\sin^2 x + 2x \sin x \cos x$

(d) $2x^2 \cos x^2 + \sin x^2$ (e) $2(x + \sin x)(1 + \cos x)$

(f) $e^x(\cos x - \sin x) + \sin x + x \cos x$ (g) $-2(2x + 3)^{-2}$

(h) $2x e^{3x} + 3x^2 e^{3x}$

4 (a) $\dfrac{dy}{dx} = e^{0.5x}(0.5 \sin x + \cos x)$

The gradient at $x = 2$ is 0.105.

(b) $\dfrac{dy}{dx} = 0.5 \sin^2 x + x \sin x \cos x$

The gradient at $x = 2$ is -0.343.

5 (a) Displacement $= 0$; velocity $= 643.4 \, \text{cm s}^{-1}$

(b) 256

6 $(x + 1)^{-1} - (x + 2)(x + 1)^{-2} = \dfrac{1}{(x + 1)} - \dfrac{(x + 2)}{(x + 1)^2}$

This is equal to $\dfrac{(x + 1) - (x + 2)}{(x + 1)^2}$ or $\dfrac{-1}{(x + 1)^2}$

2.4 Differentiating quotients

(a) Explain why $y = \dfrac{x^2}{2x + 3}$ has stationary points at $x = 0$ and $x = -3$.

(b) Evaluate the y-coordinates of the stationary points and explain why $x = -3$ gives a local maximum.

(a) $2x^2 + 6x = 0$
   $\Rightarrow x^2 + 3x = 0$
   $\Rightarrow x(x + 3) = 0$
   $\Rightarrow \qquad x = 0 \ \text{ or } \ x = -3$

(b) $x = 0 \Rightarrow y = 0$ and $x = -3 \Rightarrow y = -3$

$x = -3.1 \Rightarrow \dfrac{dy}{dx} = 0.06$ and $x = -2.9 \Rightarrow \dfrac{dy}{dx} = -0.07$

So $(-3, -3)$ is a local maximum.

EXERCISE 3

1 (a) $\dfrac{x \cos x - \sin x}{x^2}$

(b) $\dfrac{e^x(1 - x)}{e^{2x}}$ or $\dfrac{1 - x}{e^x}$

(c) $\dfrac{e^x(\sin x - \cos x)}{\sin^2 x}$

(d) $\dfrac{e^{3x}(3 \sin 2x - 2 \cos 2x)}{\sin^2 2x}$

2 (a) $\dfrac{dy}{dx} = \dfrac{e^x \cos x - e^x \sin x}{e^{2x}}$

At $x = -1$, the gradient is 3.76.

(b) $\dfrac{dy}{dx} = \dfrac{2x^2 e^{2x} - 2x e^{2x}}{x^4}$

At $x = 0.8$, the gradient is -3.87.

3 The derivative obtained by using the quotient rule is $\dfrac{-2}{(2x + 3)^2}$

and by using the chain rule it is $-2(2x + 3)^{-2}$.

The two answers are equivalent.

4 (a) $\dfrac{dy}{dx} = \dfrac{(1 + x^2) - 2x^2}{(1 + x^2)^2} = \dfrac{1 - x^2}{(1 + x^2)^2}$

At the stationary points, $1 - x^2 = 0$ so $x = \pm 1$.
When $x = -1, y = -0.5$; when $x = 1, y = 0.5$

$x = -1.1 \Rightarrow \dfrac{dy}{dx} = -0.043$ and $x = -0.9 \Rightarrow \dfrac{dy}{dx} = 0.058$,

so there is a local minimum at the point $(-1, -0.5)$.

$x = 0.9 \Rightarrow \dfrac{dy}{dx} = 0.058$ and $x = 1.1 \Rightarrow \dfrac{dy}{dx} = -0.043$,

so there is a local maximum at the point $(1, 0.5)$.

(b) $\dfrac{dy}{dx} = \dfrac{2x(x + 4) - x^2}{(x + 4)^2} = \dfrac{x^2 + 8x}{(x + 4)^2} = \dfrac{x(x + 8)}{(x + 4)^2}$

At the stationary points, $x(x + 8) = 0$, so $x = 0$ or -8.
When $x = 0, y = 0$; when $x = -8, y = -16$.

$x = -0.1 \Rightarrow \dfrac{dy}{dx} = -0.052$ and $x = 0.1 \Rightarrow \dfrac{dy}{dx} = 0.048$,

so there is a local minimum at the point $(0, 0)$.

$x = -8.1 \Rightarrow \dfrac{dy}{dx} = 0.048$ and $x = -7.9 \Rightarrow \dfrac{dy}{dx} -0.052$,

so there is a local maximum at the point $(-8, -16)$.

5 $\dfrac{\cos^2 x + \sin^2 x}{\cos^2 x} = \dfrac{1}{\cos^2 x} = \sec^2 x$

6 (a) $\dfrac{-\sin^2 x - \cos^2 x}{\sin^2 x}$ (b) $\dfrac{0 - \sec^2 x}{\tan^2 x}$

(c) Both simplify to $\dfrac{-1}{\sin^2 x}$ or $-\text{cosec}^2 x$.

7E $\dfrac{du}{dx} = y\dfrac{dv}{dx} + v\dfrac{dy}{dx}$

$v\dfrac{dy}{dx} = \dfrac{du}{dx} - y\dfrac{dv}{dx}$

$= \dfrac{du}{dx} - \dfrac{u}{v}\dfrac{dv}{dx}$

$= \dfrac{v\dfrac{du}{dx} - u\dfrac{dv}{dx}}{v}$

So $\dfrac{dy}{dx} = \dfrac{v\dfrac{du}{dx} - u\dfrac{dv}{dx}}{v^2}$

2.5 Implicit differentiation

The point $(1, 2)$ lies on the graph of $x^3 + 3y^2 - 4x + y = 11$.

(a) What is the gradient of the tangent at the point $(1, 2)$?

(b) Work out the equation of this tangent.

(a) $$x^3 + 3y^2 - 4x + y = 11$$

So $3x^2 + 6y\dfrac{dy}{dx} - 4 + \dfrac{dy}{dx} = 0$

$$\dfrac{dy}{dx}(6y + 1) = 4 - 3x^2$$

$$\dfrac{dy}{dx} = \dfrac{4 - 3x^2}{6y + 1}$$

At the point $(1, 2)$, the gradient of the tangent is $\dfrac{1}{13}$.

(b) The equation of the tangent is:

$$\dfrac{(y - 2)}{(x - 1)} = \dfrac{1}{13}$$

$13(y - 2) = x - 1$ or $13y - x = 25$

EXERCISE 4

1 (a) $4y\dfrac{dy}{dx} - 3\dfrac{dy}{dx} + 8x = 0$, so $\dfrac{dy}{dx} = \dfrac{-8x}{(4y - 3)}$

(b) $3x^2 + y\dfrac{dy}{dx} - 7 + 3\dfrac{dy}{dx} = 0$, so $\dfrac{dy}{dx} = \dfrac{(7 - 3x^2)}{(y + 3)}$

2 (a) $18x + 8y\dfrac{dy}{dx} = 0$, so $\dfrac{dy}{dx} = \dfrac{-18x}{8y}$ or $\dfrac{-9x}{4y}$

(b) When $x = 1$, $y^2 = 9$, so $y = \pm 3$
At $(1, 3)$ the gradient is -0.75.
At $(1, -3)$ the gradient is 0.75.

3 (a) $2x + 6 + 2y\dfrac{dy}{dx} - 2\dfrac{dy}{dx} = 0$

$$\dfrac{dy}{dx} = \dfrac{-(2x + 6)}{(2y - 2)}$$

At $(1, 4)$ the gradient is $-\frac{4}{3}$.

The equation of the tangent is $\dfrac{(y - 4)}{(x - 1)} = \dfrac{-4}{3}$

$$3(y - 4) = -4(x - 1)$$
$$3y + 4x = 16$$

(b) At $(1, -2)$ the gradient is $\frac{4}{3}$.
The radius joins $(1, -2)$ to $(-3, 1)$ so has gradient $-\frac{3}{4}$.
Since this is the same as $-1 \div \frac{4}{3}$ the tangent and radius are perpendicular.

(c) Other points on the circumference with integral coordinates are:

$(0, 5)$, $(0, -3)$, $(-6, 5)$, $(-7, 4)$, $(-6, -3)$ and $(-7, -2)$

At all these points the gradient of the curve should be equal to:

$$\frac{-1}{\text{gradient of radius}}$$

4   Since $x = 3 \cos \theta$ and $y = 3 \sin \theta$,

$$\frac{-x}{y} = \frac{-3 \cos \theta}{3 \sin \theta}$$

So $\dfrac{-x}{y} = \dfrac{-\cos \theta}{\sin \theta}$

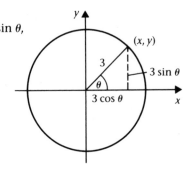

The radius joins $(0, 0)$ to (x, y),

so has gradient $\dfrac{y}{x}$.

Hence $\dfrac{-1}{(\text{gradient of radius})}$ is equal to the gradient of the tangent,

and so the radius and tangent must be perpendicular.

5   (a) $\dfrac{d}{dx}(\ln y) = \dfrac{d}{dy}(\ln y)\dfrac{dy}{dx}$,   by the chain rule

$$= \frac{1}{y}\frac{dy}{dx}$$

Now $\ln y = x \ln 2$

$$\Rightarrow \quad \frac{1}{y}\frac{dy}{dx} = \ln 2$$

$$\Rightarrow \quad \frac{dy}{dx} = y \ln 2 = \ln 2 \times 2^x$$

(b) $\dfrac{d}{dx}(3^x) = \ln 3 \times 3^x$

(c) $\dfrac{d}{dx}(a^x) = \ln a \times a^x$

2.6   Implicit differentiation and the product rule

EXERCISE 5

1   (a) $4x + 3y + 3x\dfrac{dy}{dx} - 4\dfrac{dy}{dx} + 2y\dfrac{dy}{dx} = 0$

$$(3x - 4 + 2y)\frac{dy}{dx} = -(4x + 3y)$$

$$\frac{dy}{dx} = -\frac{4x + 3y}{3x + 2y - 4}$$

(b) $2y\dfrac{dy}{dx} - 2y - 2x\dfrac{dy}{dx} + 3 - 2x = 0$

$$(2y - 2x)\dfrac{dy}{dx} = 2x + 2y - 3$$

$$\dfrac{dy}{dx} = \dfrac{2x + 2y - 3}{2y - 2x}$$

(c) $\dfrac{2 - x}{4 + 4y}$

(d) $-\dfrac{3x^2 + y^2}{2xy + 3y^2}$

2 (a) $x\dfrac{dy}{dx} + y = 0$

$$\dfrac{dy}{dx} = -\dfrac{y}{x}$$

(b) $y = \dfrac{12}{x} \Rightarrow \dfrac{dy}{dx} = -\dfrac{12}{x^2} = -\dfrac{y}{x}$

(c) –

3 (a) If $x = -2$ and $y = 3$, $x^2y + x^3 = 12 - 8 = 4$
So $(-2, 3)$ is on the curve $x^2y + x^3 = 4$.

(b) $2xy + x^2\dfrac{dy}{dx} + 3x^2 = 0$

$$\dfrac{dy}{dx} = \dfrac{-(2xy + 3x^2)}{x^2}$$

When $x = -2$ and $y = 3$, $\dfrac{dy}{dx} = \dfrac{-(-12 + 12)}{4}$, which is 0.

So $(-2, 3)$ is a stationary point on the curve.

(c) $x^2y + x^3 = 4$
$$x^2y = 4 - x^3$$
$$y = \dfrac{4 - x^3}{x^2}$$

(d) By the quotient rule:

$$\dfrac{dy}{dx} = \dfrac{x^2(-3x^2) - 2x(4 - x^3)}{x^4}$$

When $x = -2$, $\dfrac{dy}{dx} = \dfrac{(-48 + 4(4 + 8))}{4}$, which is 0.

4 (a) $3xy - 2x^2 = 8$

$$3y + 3x \frac{dy}{dx} - 4x = 0$$

$$\frac{dy}{dx} = \frac{(4x - 3y)}{3x}$$

When $x = 2$ and $y = 2\frac{2}{3}$, $\quad \frac{dy}{dx} = 0$, so $(2, 2\frac{2}{3})$ is a stationary point.

When $x = -2$ and $y = -2\frac{2}{3}$, $\quad \frac{dy}{dx} = 0$, so $(-2, -2\frac{2}{3})$ is a stationary point.

(b) $3xy - 2x^2 = 8$

$$3xy = 8 + 2x^2$$

$$y = \frac{8 + 2x^2}{3x}$$

$$\frac{dy}{dx} = \frac{12x^2 - 3(8 + 2x^2)}{9x^2} = \frac{6x^2 - 24}{9x^2}$$

At the stationary points, $6x^2 = 24$, so $x = \pm 2$.

$x = 2 \Rightarrow y = 2\frac{2}{3}$; $\quad x = -2 \Rightarrow y = -2\frac{2}{3}$, so $(2, 2\frac{2}{3})$ and $(-2, -2\frac{2}{3})$ are stationary points.

(c) It is clear that implicit differentiation is quicker for checking stationary points, but it is not well designed for finding stationary points.

3 Volume

3.1 Volume

Calculate the volume of the container when full.

The volume of the container when full is:

$$\sqrt{2} \left[\frac{2}{3}h^{1.5} + \frac{2}{5}h^{2.5} \right]_0^2 = 5.867 \, \text{m}^3$$

The (h, V) graph has the following shape:

$$V = \sqrt{2} [\frac{2}{3}h^{1.5} + \frac{2}{5}h^{2.5}]$$

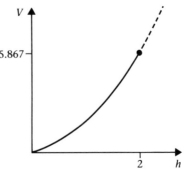

Using a graph like this, an engineer could calibrate a dipstick accurately.

3.2 Volumes of revolution

Solids can also be formed by rotating an area about an axis. Sketch the solid formed by rotating the area between the graph of $y = x^2$, the line $x = 2$ and the x-axis about the x-axis.

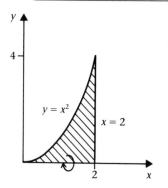

The solid will look like this:

3.3 Integration by inspection

EXERCISE 1

1 (a) $\frac{1}{3}\sin 3x + c$　　(b) $\int x^2 - 4\, dx = \frac{1}{3}x^3 - 4x + c$

 (c) $\frac{1}{5}e^{5x} + c$　　(d) $\ln |x| + c$

2 (a) $3x^2 \cos x^3$　　(b) $-4x \sin 2x^2$　　(c) $6x(x^2 - 3)^2$

3 (a) $\frac{1}{3}\sin x^3 + c$　　(b) $-\frac{1}{4}\cos 2x^2 + c$　　(c) $\frac{1}{6}(x^2 - 3)^3 + c$

4 (a)

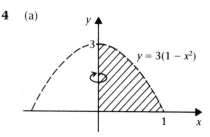

$y = 3(1 - x^2)$

(b) $V = \pi \displaystyle\int_0^3 x^2\, dy$

$$= \pi \int_0^3 1 - \tfrac{1}{3}y\, dy$$

$$= \pi \left[y - \tfrac{1}{6}y^2 \right]_0^3 = \tfrac{3}{2}\pi$$

5 (a)

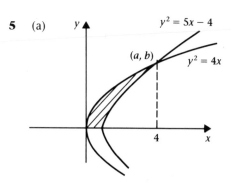

$y^2 = 5x - 4$

(a, b)

$y^2 = 4x$

At the point of intersection,
$b^2 = 5a - 4, \quad b^2 = 4a$
$\Rightarrow 4a = 5a - 4$
$\Rightarrow \quad a = 4 \quad \text{and} \quad b = 4$

(b)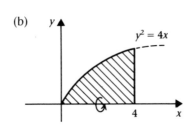

$$\text{Volume} = \pi \int_0^4 y^2 \, dx$$

$$= \pi \int_0^4 4x \, dx = 32\pi$$

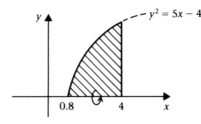

$$V = \pi \int_{0.8}^4 y^2 \, dx$$

$$= \pi \int_{0.8}^4 5x - 4 \, dx = 25.6\pi$$

The volume of material is $32\pi - 25.6\pi = 6.4\pi$ cubic units.

3.4 Integrating trigonometric functions

> Use the sum and difference formulas to prove that:
>
> (a) $2 \cos^2 x = 1 + \cos 2x$
>
> (b) $2 \sin^2 x = 1 - \cos 2x$
>
> (c) $2 \sin x \cos x = \sin 2x$

(a) $2 \cos A \cos B = \cos (A + B) + \cos (A - B)$
   Let $A = B = x$
   $\Rightarrow 2 \cos^2 x = \cos 2x + \cos 0$
   $\qquad\qquad = \cos 2x + 1$

(b) $2 \sin A \sin B = -\cos (A + B) + \cos (A - B)$
   Let $A = B = x$
   $\Rightarrow 2 \sin^2 x = -\cos 2x + \cos 0$
   $\qquad\qquad = -\cos 2x + 1$

(c) $2 \sin A \cos B = \sin (A + B) + \sin (A - B)$
   Let $A = B = x$
   $\Rightarrow 2 \sin x \cos x = \sin 2x + \sin 0$
   $\qquad\qquad\quad = \sin 2x$

E X E R C I S E   2

1 (a) $\int \sin x \cos x\, dx = \int \frac{1}{2} \sin 2x\, dx = -\frac{1}{4} \cos 2x + c$

(b) $\int \sin 3x \cos 3x\, dx = \int \frac{1}{2} \sin 6x\, dx = -\frac{1}{12} \cos 6x + c$

2 (a) $\int \cos 5x \cos x\, dx = \int \frac{1}{2} \cos 6x + \frac{1}{2} \cos 4x\, dx$

$$= \frac{1}{12} \sin 6x + \frac{1}{8} \sin 4x + c$$

(b) $\int \sin 3x \sin 7x\, dx = \int -\frac{1}{2} \cos 10x + \frac{1}{2} \cos 4x\, dx$

$$= -\frac{1}{20} \sin 10x + \frac{1}{8} \sin 4x + c$$

3 $\int_0^{\frac{1}{4}\pi} \cos^2 x\, dx = \int_0^{\frac{1}{4}\pi} (\frac{1}{2} + \frac{1}{2} \cos 2x)\, dx$

$$= \left[\frac{1}{2}x + \frac{1}{4} \sin 2x \right]_0^{\frac{1}{4}\pi}$$

$$= \frac{1}{8}\pi + \frac{1}{4}$$

4 $\pi \int_0^{\frac{1}{2}\pi} y^2\, dx = \pi \int_0^{\frac{1}{2}\pi} \sin^2 x\, dx = \frac{1}{2}\pi \int_0^{\frac{1}{2}\pi} 1 - \cos 2x\, dx$

$$= \frac{1}{2}\pi \left[x - \frac{1}{2} \sin 2x \right]_0^{\frac{1}{2}\pi} = \frac{1}{4}\pi^2$$

4 Integration techniques

4.1 Integration by parts

E X E R C I S E   1

1 (a) $xe^x - e^x + c$

(b) $\frac{1}{3}xe^{3x} - \frac{1}{9}e^{3x} + c$

(c) $\frac{1}{a} xe^{ax} - \frac{1}{a^2} e^{ax} + c$

2 (a) $x \sin x + \cos x + c$

(b) $\frac{x}{3} \sin 3x + \frac{1}{9} \cos 3x + c$

(c) $\frac{x}{a} \sin ax + \frac{1}{a^2} \cos ax + c$

3 (a) $\displaystyle\int x^2 e^x \, dx = x^2 e^x - \int 2x \, e^x \, dx$

$$= x^2 e^x - 2x e^x + 2e^x + c$$

(b) $\displaystyle\int x^2 \sin x \, dx = -x^2 \cos x + \int 2x \cos x \, dx$

$$= -x^2 \cos x + 2x \sin x + 2 \cos x + c$$

4 (a) Put $u = x \Rightarrow \dfrac{du}{dx} = 1$ and $\dfrac{dv}{dx} = \sin 2x \Rightarrow v = -\tfrac{1}{2}\cos 2x$

$$\int_{-1}^{0} x \sin 2x \, dx = \left[-\tfrac{1}{2}x \cos 2x \right]_{-1}^{0} - \int_{-1}^{0} 1(-\tfrac{1}{2}\cos 2x) \, dx$$

$$\approx 0 + 0.20807 + \left[\tfrac{1}{4}\sin 2x \right]_{-1}^{0} \approx 0.44$$

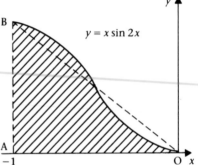

The area found is shaded in the diagram.
When $x = -1$, $x \sin 2x \approx 0.91$

The shaded area is close to that of triangle AOB $\approx \tfrac{1}{2} \times 0.91 \times 1 = 0.455$, which indicates that the answer is reasonable.

(b) Put $u = 2x \Rightarrow \dfrac{du}{dx} = 2$ and $\dfrac{dv}{dx} = e^{0.5x} \Rightarrow v = 2e^{0.5x}$

$$\int_{-3}^{0} 2x e^{0.5x} \, dx = \left[2x \times 2e^{0.5x} \right]_{-3}^{0} - \int_{-3}^{0} 2 \times 2e^{0.5x} \, dx$$

$$\approx 0 + 2.6776 - \left[8e^{0.5x} \right]_{-3}^{0} \approx 2.6776 - 8 + 1.7850 \approx -3.54$$

The area found is shaded in the diagram.
The minimum value, -1.47, of $2x e^{0.5x}$ is between $x = -3$ and $x = 0$.
An estimate of the shaded area is approximately
$-2\tfrac{1}{2} \times 1.47 \approx -3.67$(negative because it is below the x-axis), which indicates that the answer is reasonable.

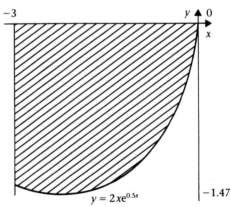

4.2 Integration by substitution

E X E R C I S E   2

1 (a) $u = x + 3 \Rightarrow \dfrac{du}{dx} = 1$

$\displaystyle\int u^5 \, du = \frac{1}{6}u^6 + c$

$= \frac{1}{6}(x + 3)^6 + c$

(b) $u = 2x - 5 \Rightarrow \dfrac{du}{dx} = 2$

$\displaystyle\int \frac{1}{2}(u + 5)\, u^6 \, \frac{1}{2}\, du = \frac{1}{4}\int (u^7 + 5u^6)\, du$

$= \frac{1}{32}u^8 + \frac{5}{28}u^7 + c$

$= \frac{1}{32}(2x - 5)^8 + \frac{5}{28}(2x - 5)^7 + c$

(c) $\displaystyle\int (u + 2)^2\, u^7 \, du = \int (u^9 + 4u^8 + 4u^7)\, du$

$= \frac{1}{10}(x - 2)^{10} + \frac{4}{9}(x - 2)^9 + \frac{1}{2}(x - 2)^8 + c$

(d) $\frac{1}{18}(x^2 - 4)^9 + c$

(e) $\frac{2}{9}(x^3 - 2)^{\frac{3}{2}} + c$

2 (a) $\frac{1}{3}\sin^3 x + c$ (b) $-\frac{1}{3}\cos^3 x + c$

3 (a) Let $u = x^3 + 3 \Rightarrow \dfrac{du}{dx} = 3x^2.$ Replace dx by $\dfrac{1}{3x^2}\, du.$

$\displaystyle\int x^2 \, \sqrt{(x^3 + 3)} \, dx = \int x^2 \, \sqrt{(x^3 + 3)} \, \frac{1}{3x^2}\, du$

$= \displaystyle\int \frac{1}{3}u^{\frac{1}{2}} \, du$

$= \frac{2}{9}u^{\frac{3}{2}} + c$

$= \frac{2}{9}(x^3 + 3)^{\frac{3}{2}} + c$

(b) $\frac{1}{7}(x - 3)^7 + \frac{1}{2}(x - 3)^6 + c$

(c) Let $u = x - 2 \Rightarrow \dfrac{du}{dx} = 1.$ Replace dx by du and x by $u + 2.$

$\displaystyle\int x \, \sqrt{(x - 2)}\, dx = \int (u + 2)\, \sqrt{u}\, du$

$= \displaystyle\int u^{1\frac{1}{2}} + 2u^{\frac{1}{2}}\, du$

$= \frac{2}{5}u^{2\frac{1}{2}} + \frac{4}{3}u^{1\frac{1}{2}}$

$= \frac{2}{5}(x - 2)^{2\frac{1}{2}} + \frac{4}{3}(x - 2)^{1\frac{1}{2}}$

(d) $\frac{1}{4}\sin^4 x + c$

(e) Let $u = \cos x \Rightarrow \dfrac{du}{dx} = -\sin x$. Replace $\sin x\, dx$ by $-du$.

$$\int \cos^5 x \sin x\, dx = -\int u^5\, du$$
$$= -\tfrac{1}{6}u^6 + c$$
$$= -\tfrac{1}{6}\cos^6 x + c$$

(f) Let $u = x + 2 \Rightarrow \dfrac{du}{dx} = 1$. Replace x by $u - 2$ and dx by du.

$$\int \frac{x}{(x+2)^3}\, dx = \int \frac{u-2}{u^3}\, du$$
$$= \int (u^{-2} - 2u^{-3})\, du$$
$$= -u^{-1} + u^{-2} + c$$
$$= \frac{1}{(x+2)^2} - \frac{1}{(x+2)} + c$$

4.3 The reciprocal function

Use the method of substitution to show that: ·
$$\int \frac{f'(x)}{f(x)}\, dx = \int \frac{1}{u}\, du \quad \text{if } u = f(x)$$

If $u = f(x)$ then $\dfrac{du}{dx} = f'(x)$ and $\dfrac{dx}{du} = \dfrac{1}{f'(x)}$

The variable of the integral can be changed from x to u by replacing dx by $\dfrac{dx}{du}\, du$. So

$$\int \frac{f'(x)}{f(x)}\, dx = \int \frac{f'(x)}{f(x)} \times \frac{1}{f'(x)}\, du = \int \frac{1}{f(x)}\, du = \int \frac{1}{u}\, du$$

Why is it not possible to evaluate $\displaystyle\int_{-a}^{a} \frac{1}{x}\, dx$?

Because there is a vertical asymptote at $x = 0$. (The function is not defined for $x = 0$.) Always look carefully at your function to see that it is defined for all values of x within the interval of the limits.

EXERCISE 3

1 (a) $3 \ln|x - 2| + c$ (b) $3 \ln|2x + 7| + c$ (c) $\frac{1}{3} \ln|3x - 1| + c$

2 (a) $\frac{2}{3} \ln|4| - \frac{2}{3} \ln|1| = 0.9242$ (to 4 d.p.)

  (b) $\frac{2}{3} \ln|-5| - \frac{2}{3} \ln|-8| = -0.3133$ (to 4 d.p.)

3 The function is not defined for $x = 2$.

4 (a) $\displaystyle\int \frac{\sin x}{\cos x} \, dx = -\ln|\cos x| = \ln|(\cos x)^{-1}| = \ln|\sec x| + c$

  (b) $\displaystyle\int \frac{\cos x}{\sin x} \, dx = \ln|\sin x| + c$

4.4 Partial fractions

Use a similar method to find $\displaystyle\int \frac{4x - 3}{2x + 1} \, dx$.

$$\frac{4x - 3}{2x + 1} = \frac{4x + 2 - 5}{2x + 1} = 2 - \frac{5}{2x + 1}$$

$$\int 2 - \frac{5}{2x + 1} \, dx = \int 2 \, dx - \frac{5}{2} \int \frac{2}{2x + 1} \, dx = 2x - \frac{5}{2} \ln|2x + 1| + c$$

EXERCISE 4

1 (a) $\dfrac{3}{x + 3} - \dfrac{2}{x + 2}$ (b) $\dfrac{6}{2x + 1} - \dfrac{3}{x + 1}$ (c) $\dfrac{3}{2x - 1} - \dfrac{1}{x + 2}$

  (d) $\dfrac{5}{x - 1} + \dfrac{2}{x - 2}$ (e) $\dfrac{3}{2x + 1} - \dfrac{2}{3x + 2}$ (f) $\dfrac{2}{x + 1} - \dfrac{1}{x}$

2 (a) $\dfrac{2}{x + 3} + \dfrac{3}{x - 4}$

  (b) $2 \ln|x + 3| + 3 \ln|x - 4| + c$

3 $\dfrac{x^2 + 3x + 2 + 5x + 7}{x^2 + 3x + 2} = 1 + \dfrac{5x + 7}{x^2 + 3x + 2} = 1 + \dfrac{2}{x + 1} + \dfrac{3}{x + 2}$

$$\int_0^1 1 + \frac{2}{x + 1} + \frac{3}{x + 2} \, dx = \left[x + 2 \ln|x + 1| + 3 \ln|x + 2| \right]_0^1 = 3.6027 \quad \text{(to 4 d.p.)}$$

5 Polynomial approximations

5.1 Taylor's first approximation

Plot the function on a graph plotter and superimpose Taylor's first approximation. For what range of values is the approximation a good one?

What counts as good is very much a matter of opinion. If good is taken to mean that the approximation gives an error of no more than 5%, then $0.31 < x < 0.84$.

EXERCISE 1

1 (a) $\dfrac{dy}{dx} = 3x^2 + 5$

The gradient at $x = 2$ is 17.

$\dfrac{y - 16}{x - 2} = 17$ gives $y = 17x - 18$.

(b) $y = x + 1$

(c) $y = x - 1$

(d) $y = 28x - 44$

(e) $y = 3x - 2$

2E (a) $y = -x + \frac{1}{2}\pi$

(b) 0.070796

(c) 0.084%

5.2 The Newton–Raphson method

EXERCISE 2

1 Using $x_{n+1} = x_n - \dfrac{x_n - \cos x_n}{1 + \sin x_n}$ with $x_1 = 1$, then $x_2 = 0.750364 \ldots$ and
$x = 0.739085 \ldots$ You can see that there is only one solution by plotting the graphs of $y = x$ and $y = \cos x$ on the same axes. They will only intersect at one point.

2 $x^3 = 3x - 1 \Rightarrow x \approx 1.532089, \quad 0.347296 \quad$ or $\quad -1.879385$

3 $x = 0.487404$

4   The area of sector OACB is $\frac{1}{2}\theta r^2$.
Triangle OAB is isosceles and has area $r^2 \sin \frac{1}{2}\theta \cos \frac{1}{2}\theta = \frac{1}{2}r^2 \sin \theta$.

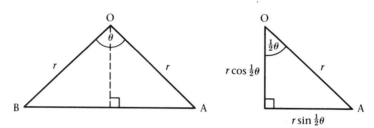

Hence the area of the segment $\frac{1}{2}\theta r^2 - \frac{1}{2}r^2 \sin \theta = \frac{1}{10}\pi r^2$.
$\Rightarrow \theta - \frac{1}{5}\pi = \sin \theta$
$\theta = 1.627$ to 3 decimal places

5E   (a) $2\theta r^2 - r^2 \sin 2\theta$

(b) $\theta = 0.8832$

6E   (a) (i) Jerry

(ii) Tom – exponential growth will always outperform quadratic growth eventually.

(b) 19.03 years, i.e. 19 years 0 months

5.3   Quadratic approximations

> If $f(x) = \cos x$, then $f(0) = 1$, $f'(0) = 0$ and $f''(0) = -1$. Find the quadratic function $p(x) = a + bx + cx^2$ for which $p(0) = 1$, $p'(0) = 0$ and $p''(0) = -1$.

$1 = p(0) = a$, $0 = p'(0) = b$, $-1 = p''(0) = 2c$
$\Rightarrow p(x) = 1 - \frac{1}{2}x^2$
If you plot $y = 1 - \frac{1}{2}x^2$ on the same axes as $y = \cos x$, you will see how good an approximation this is. (Remember to work in radians.)

> Find the quadratic approximation to $f(x) = e^x$ at $x = 0$.

$f(x) = f'(x) = f''(x) = e^x \Rightarrow f(0) = 1$, $f'(0) = 1$ and $f''(0) = 1$
The quadratic approximation $p(x) = a + bx + cx^2$ will be such that:

$1 = p(0) = a$, $1 = p'(0) = b$ and $1 = p''(0) = 2c$
$\Rightarrow p(x) = 1 + x + \frac{1}{2}x^2$

If you plot $y = 1 + x + \frac{1}{2}x^2$ on the same axes as $y = e^x$, you will see how good an approximation this is.

109

5.4 Maclaurin's series

What value does this suggest 0! should have? Check your suggestion using a calculator.

Comparing the series $f(0) + f'(0) x + \dfrac{f''(0)x^2}{2!} + \dots$

with $\dfrac{f(0)x^0}{0!} + \dfrac{f'(0)x^1}{1!} + \dfrac{f''(0)x^2}{2!} + \dots$

0! must be equal to 1.

Although this seems most unlikely, there are several instances in mathematics where the logical consequence of extending a pattern to include 0! makes it necessary to define 0! as 1. Try evaluating 0! on your calculator and you will get the answer 1.

(a) Use a graph plotter to superimpose the graphs of:

$$y = \sin x \quad \text{and} \quad y = x - \frac{x^3}{3!} + \frac{x^5}{5!} - \frac{x^7}{7!} + \frac{x^9}{9!}$$

How good an approximation is the polynomial to the sine wave?

(b) Explain why $\cos x = 1 - \dfrac{x^2}{2!} + \dfrac{x^4}{4!} - \dfrac{x^6}{6!} + \dots$

(c) Find the series for e^x.

(a) The approximation as it stands is good for all values of x from -3.6 to 3.6. By adding further terms to the series the approximation can be made as good as is necessary for any desired range of x.

(b) $f(x) = \cos x \quad \Rightarrow \quad f(0) = 1$
$f'(x) = - \sin x \Rightarrow f'(0) = 0$
$f''(x) = - \cos x \Rightarrow f''(0) = -1$
$f^{(3)}(x) = \sin x \quad \Rightarrow \quad f^{(3)}(0) = 0$
$f^{(4)}(x) = \cos x \quad \Rightarrow \quad f^{(4)}(0) = 1$

and the cycle repeats itself.

$$\Rightarrow \cos x = 1 + 0x + \frac{(-1)x^2}{2!} + \frac{0x^3}{3!} + \frac{1x^4}{4!} + \frac{0x^5}{5!} + \frac{(-1)x^6}{6!} \dots$$

$$= 1 - \frac{x^2}{2!} + \frac{x^4}{4!} - \frac{x^6}{6} + \dots$$

(c) $f(x) = e^x \Rightarrow f(0) = 1$
$f'(x) = e^x \Rightarrow f'(0) = 1$

and it is clear that all derivatives will take the value 1 when $x = 0$.

$$\Rightarrow e^x = 1 + x + \frac{x^2}{2!} + \frac{x^3}{3!} + \frac{x^4}{4!} + \dots$$

EXERCISE 3

1 (a) $f(x) = e^{2x}$, $f'(x) = 2e^{2x}$, $f''(x) = 4e^{2x}$, etc.
$f(0) = 1$, $f'(0) = 2$, $f''(0) = 4$, etc.

$\Rightarrow e^{2x} = 1 + 2x + \dfrac{4x^2}{2!} + \dfrac{8x^3}{3!} + \dfrac{16x^4}{4!} + \ldots$

(b) Replacing x by $2x$ in $e^x = 1 + x + \dfrac{x^2}{2!} + \ldots$

gives $e^{2x} = 1 + (2x) + \dfrac{(2x)^2}{2!} + \dfrac{(2x)^3}{3!} + \dfrac{(2x)^4}{4!}$

$= 1 + 2x + \dfrac{4x^2}{2!} + \dfrac{8x^3}{3!} + \dfrac{16x^4}{4!} + \ldots$

2 By taking the first 15 terms of the series, $e = 2.718\,281\,828\,459$ to 12 decimal places.

3 (a) $0.877\,582\,5619$

(b) $1 - \dfrac{0.5^2}{2!} = 0.875$

$1 - \dfrac{0.5^2}{2!} + \dfrac{0.5^4}{4!} = 0.8776$ so three terms are needed.

(c) $\cos 1.0 = 0.540\,302\,3059$

$1 - \dfrac{1}{2!} + \dfrac{1}{4!} = 0.541\,67$

$1 - \dfrac{1}{2!} + \dfrac{1}{4!} - \dfrac{1}{6!} = 0.540\,28$ so four terms are needed.

4 (a) $\dfrac{x^{n-1}}{(n-1)!}$ (b) $(-1)^{n-1}\dfrac{x^{2n-2}}{(2n-2)!}$ (c) $\dfrac{x^{2n-2}}{(n-1)!}$

5 (a) Replacing x by $-x$ in the series for $\ln(1+x)$ gives:

$$\ln(1-x) = -x - \dfrac{x^2}{2} - \dfrac{x^3}{3} - \dfrac{x^4}{4} \ldots$$

(b) $\ln(1-x^2) = \ln(1-x)(1+x) = \ln(1-x) + \ln(1+x)$

$$= 2\left(-\dfrac{x^2}{2} - \dfrac{x^4}{4} - \dfrac{x^6}{6} \ldots\right) = -x^2 - \dfrac{x^4}{2} - \dfrac{x^6}{3} \ldots$$

6 (a) –

(b) $\sqrt{(1 - e^{-x})} \approx \sqrt{(1 - (1 - x))} = \sqrt{x}$

(c) $\sqrt{0.1} = 0.3162$

$\sqrt{(1 - e^{-0.1})} = 0.3085 \Rightarrow$ percentage error $= 2.5\%$

6 First principles

6.1 Zooming in

> Use a graph plotter to plot the graph of:
>
> $$y = x + \tfrac{1}{1000}\sin(1000x)$$
>
> Investigate what happens as you zoom in on any point of the graph.

With 'normal' scales, the graph looks like that
of $y = x$, with gradient 1 at all points.

As you zoom in, the fact that a sine curve
has been superimposed on the line $y = x$
becomes clear.

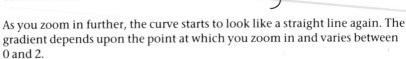

As you zoom in further, the curve starts to look like a straight line again. The
gradient depends upon the point at which you zoom in and varies between
0 and 2.

6.3 Differentiating from first principles

EXERCISE 1

1 (a) $\displaystyle\lim_{h\to0}\frac{3(1+h)^2-3}{h} = \lim_{h\to0}\frac{\cancel{3}+6h+3h^2-\cancel{3}}{h}$

$$= \lim_{h\to0}\ (6+3h) = 6$$

(b) $\displaystyle\frac{dy}{dx} = \lim_{h\to0}\frac{3(x+h)^2-3x^2}{h}$

$$= \lim_{h\to0}\ (6x+3h) = 6x$$

2 $\displaystyle\lim_{h\to0}\frac{[5(x+h)^2+3(x+h)]-[5x^2+3x]}{h} = 10x+3$

3 $\displaystyle\lim_{h\to0}\frac{[4(x+h)^2-2(x+h)+7]-[4x^2-2x+7]}{h} = 8x-2$

4E $\displaystyle\lim_{h\to0}\frac{\sin(x+h)-\sin x}{h} = \lim_{h\to0}\frac{\sin x\cos h+\cos x\sin h-\sin x}{h}$

$$= \lim_{h\to0}\left[\frac{\cos h-1}{h}\sin x+\frac{\sin h}{h}\cos x\right]$$

$$= 0\times\sin x+1\times\cos x = \cos x$$